Stan Jarvis
Drawings by Jane Hannath

Around Historic Essex

MIDAS BOOKS

Tilbury Hailing Station

The Illustrator

Jane Hannath was born in Salisbury, Rhodesia in 1954. She came to England in 1973, where she attended Maidstone College of Art in Kent and left in 1976 with a BA in Art and Design. She now lives in Tunbridge Wells and would like to devote her life entirely to drawings, films and food.

First published 1979 by
MIDAS Books
12 Dene Way, Speldhurst,
Tunbridge Wells, Kent TN3 0NX

© Stan Jarvis and Jane Hannath 1979

ISBN 0 85936 165 9

Printed by photolithography and bound in Great Britain at The Pitman Press, Bath.

CONTENTS AND ILLUSTRATIONS

ALDHAM

Aldham gives a name to a number of hamlets and a village on quiet back lanes spreading south from the river Colne where it is crossed by the A604. Near the cross roads is the church of St Margaret and St Catherine which is not remarkable in itself, for it was built in 1855 to replace the ruinous original church a mile away. The 14th-century wooden south porch was in fact moved here from the old church, but the most interesting feature, inside the church, is a tombstone brought back from the wilderness of the old churchyard and set up as a permanent memorial to a great man of Essex. It is inscribed: 'Beneath this stone are deposited the remains of the Revd. Philip Morant, A.M., 25 years Rector of this parish. Died November 25th 1770 aged 70. Also of Anne his wife, died July 28th 1767, aged 69.' A further inscription tells us that the stone was recovered and restored by the Essex Archaeological Society in 1966. Philip Morant, born in Jersey in 1700, was sent to school in England and from University took up a curacy in Great Waltham under a noted historian of the day, Doctor Nicholas Tindal, who set him a fine example in historical research and writing. He moved around the county from living to living and married an Essex heiress, Anne Stebbing of Great Tey, but not until he was 39. He was 45 when he came to his last appointment, as Rector of Aldham. Three years later he had published, by private subscription, *The History and Antiquities of Colchester*. After years of further work on revising and adding to a collection of the writings of a number of unsuccessful authors of Essex histories Morant was able to produce a second edition of his book on Colchester as the first part of the larger, *History and Antiquities of the County of Essex*, which appeared in parts over eight years from 1760.

Though Philip Morant's remains still lie in the old churchyard at Aldham it is good to know that a leading county society was instrumental in remounting his tombstone and dedicating a window in appreciation of the great contribution this humble Rector made to the proper recording of our county's history.

ARKESDEN

One of the prettiest villages in the Uttlesford District lies west of the A11 in the northwest corner of the county. Cottages, many of them thatched, gather round the green and along the banks of the diminutive stream, a winter bourne, called Wicken Water. The church of St Mary was much restored in 1855 but nave and chancel are of the 13th century. Of many interesting features one is the tomb to Richard Cutte who died in 1592, and Mary his wife. Under a canopy supported by six leaf-carved columns their effigies lie recumbent on a tomb chest which shows, in arched recesses on the side, their children kneeling in pious respect.

It was a later member of this family, John Cutts, born here in 1661, who made the name famous for fearless fighting in the service of his country. Swift said he was, 'as brave and brainless as the sword he wears' and he was known among his contemporaries as the 'Salamander' because he survived so many hot encounters with the enemy in campaigns all over Europe. He died in 1707 largely from the cumulative effect of the many wounds he had received in battle.

ASHDON 1

Ashdon borders on Cambridgeshire but keeps much of the charm of an old Essex village. The ancient settlement grew around the church at the top of the hill with more recent development in the valley of the Bourne stream. In between, to south and east down the hill can be detected the terraces on which the vanished homes of the early settlement once stood.

By the small green in the vale stands the Guildhall, now a private house, built about 1480 to the order of the Guild of St Mary. It owes its present fine condition to a thorough restoration from an almost derelict state in 1960, having descended through the years to the status of a poorhouse and ultimately three wretched tenements.

The Rose and Crown is a hostelry which can prove its origin in the early 17th century by the unusual geometric wall painting still surviving in one of the bars; panels are filled with flowing arabesques in black, red and white.

ASHDON 2

In the north of the parish can be seen the Bartlow Hills, four huge burial mounds surviving from the eight originally raised, said to be the largest in Europe, reaching as much as 45ft high and 144ft in diameter. One has been separated from the others by the railway. They were excavated as early as 1840 and pronounced to be of the late 1st or early 2nd century AD.

The cremated remains of some unidentified ancient British tribal chiefs (including, some say, Boadicea herself) were contained in glass vessels placed in wood- or tile-lined chambers deep in the mounds, accompanied by bronze, glass and earthenware vessels holding food and wine for the long journey to the after-life. But it would have been better if they had never seen the light of day, for they were kept by Lord Maynard at Easton Lodge and were lost in the fire which engulfed it in 1847, except for just a few objects now in the Saffron Walden Museum.

Bartlow Hills taken from an old print

ASHELDAM

'The good news is that Jesus died, was buried and rose again. We have some more good news. Asheldam Church "died", "was buried" and "will rise again" and you can be part of it.' These opening sentences of an article in the *Essex Churchman* preface an interesting story.

It begins in the days when an Ancient British tribe made a clearing in the forest and levelled it to form a characteristic defensible plateau camp, now only just detectable some 600yds west of the church. At some time another earthwork was thrown up to enclose a 16acre oval within which Church and Hall now stand. The Saxons may well have built the first church in that increasing settlement. When it was rebuilt in the early 14th century the *Roman* bricks still lying about were incorporated in the massive tower to which brick battlements were later added.

Unostentatiously but significantly, the Church of St Lawrence served its community through six hundred years, until the day came when its maintenance and repair could no longer be supported by a diminished congregation. It was 'declared redundant' in 1968 and stood for eight years in decaying uselessness at the mercy of vandals. Then it came to the attention of the Diocesan Youth Centre in its search for 'a place where holiness and adventure — both unlimited — could come together in youth and hope'. Through voluntary labour St Lawrence's was revitalised, though the old congregation would be surprised to see the bunk beds for twenty in the nave and a fully-equipped kitchen and lavatories which have been added.

Now Asheldham Youth Church provides a place where 'twenty youngsters, of all denominations, who might find Christ there can "get away from it all" and enjoy together times of adventure, fellowship, fun, prayer, worship and love'.

AUDLEY END

'Too large for a King, though it might do for a Lord Treasurer, ...' So King James is supposed to have commented on viewing the great mansion of Audley End, a mile west of the centre of Saffron Walden. The Lord Treasurer would be parallelled today to the Chancellor of the Exchequer. In 1614 that office was filled by the Earl of Suffolk, formerly Baron Howard of Walden, and rumour has it that he filled his purse at the same time, for he was dismissed in disgrace in 1618. Much of his wealth was poured out in building one of the largest houses in the kingdom, comparing easily with Hampton Court in size and splendour. There is a mystery about Audley End — all the records of its building are unaccountably lost, so it can only be deduced that it was begun in 1603 and finished in 1616, the cost being something like ten million pounds by today's values.

Its size was far larger than the existing mansion; from a huge gatehouse with four towers one approached a massive pile which completely enclosed two courtyards in a design, by Bernard Johnson, which was a watershed of the Anglo-Flemish style. But from the day it was built it was a millstone round the family's neck, for it was too big to be completely occupied or fully furnished, though the Earl, disgraced as he was, lived there until his death in 1626. The family continued in residence until Charles II took a fancy to it and bought it for £50,000 in 1669 but because he was unable to pay the whole sum, Audley End reverted to the family in 1701.

By 1720 three sides of the outer court had been demolished and in another thirty years further demolitions reduced the mansion to its present, still-imposing size. Its present condition is largely due to a £100,000 overhaul by a later owner, Lord Braybrooke, at the end of the 18th century. It finally passed into national ownership in 1948, though the contents are still owned by the family. The house and gardens, the latter landscaped by Capability Brown, are open to the general public and a full guide is available.

BARKING 1

Though it is a London Borough now, it was for so long an important Essex fishing port, not closed until 1899, that it must find a place in any book on Essex. Its Abbey, founded in about 666 by Erkenwald, later Bishop of London, was renowned for its wealth. Razed by the Danes, it was rebuilt by King Edgar in 970 and lived in by William the Conqueror while his Tower of London was building. But six hundred years of history meant nothing to Henry VIII — it was all demolished by his Commissioners in 1541 and re-used in royal palaces at Greenwich and Deptford.

Just one part of that old Abbey remains in the shape of the Fire Bell, or Curfew Tower. It was rebuilt for the second time around 1460. In those days the parish church of St Margaret's did not have a bell tower, so the Abbess allowed this part of her Abbey to be used as a belfry, standing as it did across the path to the church from the east. Its value to the town as a fire and curfew bell excepted it from the general destruction so it stands today as the Town Gate, entrance to, and guardian of the peace of the parish church in which Captain Cook was married in 1762, summed up by Ian Nairn as 'A happy rambling town church ... One of everything, from a fragment of a Saxon cross onwards ...'

11

BARKING 2

Eastbury House: What tales could be told by the walls and windows of this family home, built in 1572, with typical Tudor chimneys, tall and ornate, to announce its ancestry. Protests by local people prevented its demolition in Victorian times and again before World War I, during which it was occupied by the soldiery. The National Trust was able to acquire it in 1920, but it continued in use as an ex-servicemen's club until the early 30s, when it was left unoccupied and suffered damage. From 1934, when it was restored and opened as a museum, it has been leased to the local authority and used successively as a Civil Defence post, a day nursery and an Occupation Centre.

Clement Sysley who purchased the manor in 1557 and had the house built, hoped that it would remain in the family 'for ever', but it passed into other hands within thirty years of his death. The very variety of uses to which it has been put has helped in the preservation of this 'very valuable example of a medium-sized Elizabethan manor house' as the expert Nikolaus Pevsner describes it. Tradition has it that the conspirators in the Gunpowder Plot held their secret meetings here and arranged to view the explosion from the top of the house, but there is no substantiation.

BARKINGSIDE

In a ninety-year-old guide the whole history of this modern suburb gets just two lines, followed by four lines noting: 'Here is Dr Barnardo's Village Home for Destitute Girls. The inmates, numbering about 600, are accommodated in 30 separate houses arranged in a square. Others are in the course of erection. The matrons are chiefly ladies who voluntarily give their services.' That shows how famous these homes had become in a mere eight years from their inception as four cottages in 1873, set in gardens within walking distance of the busy Gants Hill junction of the North Circular Road and the A12.

Dr Thomas John Barnado, born in 1845, purposefully resolved at the age of 17 to spend his life helping others, and was soon directed to the plight of poor, parentless children left to fend for themselves in the slums of the great towns. When he founded the East End Mission for Destitute Children in 1867 he was just 22. Three years later his Boys' Home at Stepney was opened. When he was given Mossford Lodge, Barkingside, as a wedding present he had the rear of the house adapted to house 60 girls. By 1879 there were 24 cottages dotted about the grounds. When Barnardo died in 1905 there were 64 houses giving 1300 girls a place they could really call home. Today Mossford Lodge is the administrative centre of a national network of children's homes.

It is fitting that the ashes of the founder should be buried in his village Children's Church, under a simple monument designed by Sir George Frampton. It is said by Sir William Addison: 'At the time of his death it was estimated that Dr Barnardo had helped a quarter of a million children.' Small wonder, then, that this hard-working 'step-father' has been quoted as saying: 'I have never seen an ugly child.'

Dr. Barnardo and his Boys' Home   13

BATTLESBRIDGE

Some folk have found a connection between the name of this village and the Battle of Ashingdon at which Canute beat Edmund Ironside in 1016, but Ashingdon is a good five miles east of this hamlet, which stands on the banks of the tidal Crouch. Its bridge was very important and had to be kept in good repair by the local squire, and as the Bataille family fulfilled that function in the 14th century it is more than likely that the bridge was named after them.

It has been built time and again as floods of water, and later floods of traffic, battered away at it. In recent times the County Council has left signs of its handiwork in the form of seaxes on the bridge supports. Nearby on the south bank an old brick building exhibits evidence of its origin as a tidal mill. There are two, tall, gaunt mills standing either side of the bridge but neither is now working to its original purpose.

Where the busy quayside saw so much bustle of barge and cart traffic, the cars now draw up to drop the pleasure-seeking loads of passengers at 'The Barge'.

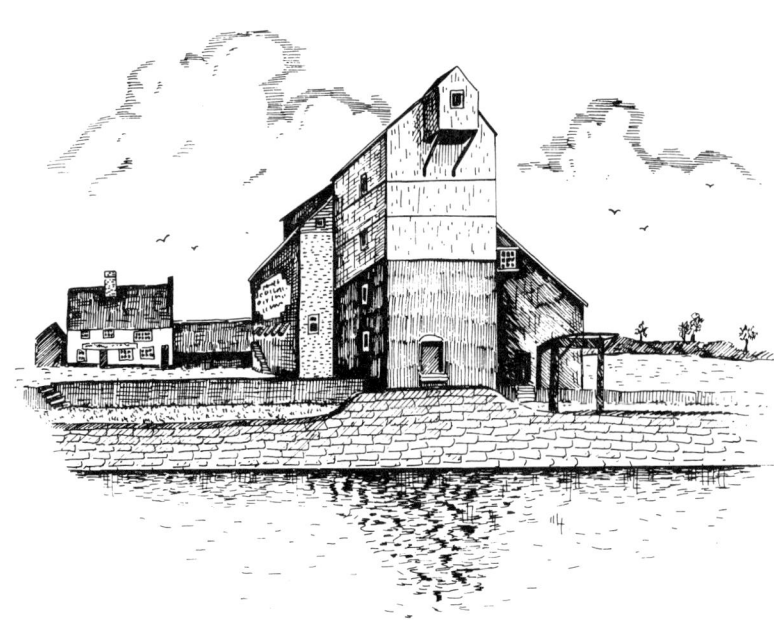

BEAUCHAMP RODING

There are eight villages which take half their names from the little river Roding – the very reason for settlement here in Saxon times. This particular village has a curious claim to our attention. The church stands in the fields as though it has drawn apart from the village which looks up to its 15th-century tower and beyond to the B184. Inside St Botolph's can be seen a complete staircase to the rood loft; one of very few to escape the hammers of the Puritans.

The curiosity is to be found where the drive to the farm called 'Hornets' meets the lane. In a triangular wilderness of nettles and brambles can be seen crosses and a big memorial stone marking the resting places of the Mead family. Isaac Mead was a self-made man. From a poor country boy, born in 1859, who started work at eleven years old milking cows six days a week, and through a life of hard work during all the daylight hours he became a farmer and a landowner. It was his wish that he and his family should be buried in a corner of the land which had succoured them in life. His wife pre-deceased him and his sons followed him to the grave, and all his achievements would be forgotten but for his written account in *The Life Story of an Essex Lad*, published in 1923 and now a collector's item.

BEELEIGH ABBEY

Books, thousands of them, line the library walls; not surprising, for the Abbey has been owned for years by the Foyle family of London bookshop fame. There were very few books indeed to be had when the Abbey was founded in 1170 by Sir Robert de Mantel of whom a tentative statue has been erected on the lawn behind the present house. The complex of old Abbey outbuildings and the Tudor house stand on a lane off the back road from Danbury to Maldon. Past the Abbey the lane stops at the river bank, a pleasant picnic spot.

Visitors to the Abbey and its beautiful gardens can obtain a very useful guide which explains the origin of the monastery of St Mary and St Nicholas as the house of the only community of white canons in Essex, a cell of the French Premonstratensian order, which was suppressed in 1536. The calefactory, or warming room, is now a living room of great beauty, with a ceiling vaulted like that of the adjacent chapterhouse, which serves the modern owners as a chapel where there is an organ which belonged to Handel. The climax of a visit for book-lovers must be the sight of that collection of rare and beautiful books in the peaceful atmosphere of the room where once the monks were wont to sleep.

BERNERS RODING

The tiny church whose dedication has long since been forgotten is just nave and chancel beneath a weather-boarded belfry. It shows 16th-century origin in its chancel windows, and stands behind Berners Hall which, with two or three houses, forms the nucleus of this village down a narrow lane which leads to nowhere but the fields south of the A414 at Pepper's Green. This land was held at the Domesday Survey by Hugh de Berners; the family continued to inhabit the Hall, and Coller notes in his history of 1861: 'Sir James Berners, the proprietor of Berners Hall, was beheaded, as one of the evil councillors of Richard II, when the estate was con-fiscated ... Juliana Berners, one of the fast women of the day, the daughter of Sir James, was born here ...' That was some time before 1388 and the girl grew up to be a fun-loving courtier who became eventually the Prioress of Sopwell nunnery at St Albans where she distilled her experience of court life and outdoor activity on her father's estate here in Essex into a manuscript entitled *Treatyse perteynynge to Hawkynge, Huntynge, Fysshynge, and Coot Armiris*. It is likely that our authoress actually wrote only the section on hunting and part of that on hawking, the two pursuits of which she would have had intimate knowledge. The whole work became one of the first books printed in English in 1486, by Wynkyn de Worde.

BILLERICAY 1

In a High Street much altered by recent building and restoration one old house with exposed timbers draws the eye. Chantry House stands opposite the church of St Mary Magdalene. It was built in 1510 in conjunction with houses beside it, now numbered separately, as a hall house which predates even the Tudor brick church tower. Billericay is rich in old houses but Chantry House has the added attraction of association with one of the redoubtable Pilgrim Fathers, Christopher Martin.

He was a miller in this town, and treasurer to that amazing group of people who decided to move to a distant country across an unknown ocean that they might practise their religious beliefs without persecution. Martin married the widow Mary Prower in the parish church, but their protestant faith caused them to join the independent church in Chelmsford and then to flee to Holland to join the growing movement there. From Holland in 1619 the group sent Martin and two other men back to England to look for a ship for their great voyage, and they found the Mayflower. They brought it round to Leigh and provisioned it, and set off in the summer of 1620. It was a miracle that Christopher Martin and Mary, together with brother Solomon Prower and servant John Langerman, survived the long, hard journey and a tragedy that all the Billericay contingent should die during the first winter while they were still living on board ship off the Massachusetts coast.

So much of that momentous undertaking must have been discussed over and over again within the walls of Chantry House in which Christopher Martin is reliably reputed to have lived.

Chantry House

BILLERICAY 2

Norsey Wood, which spreads north-east from the heart of Billericay, is still an open space, though pressed on three sides now by residential development. It was a larger wood altogether, with hardly a house in sight when its name was written indelibly in the history books back in 1381.

Life had become so hard for the labouring classes that they rose in revolt, the Peasants Revolt. The King bravely met the Essex rebels assembled at Mile End and dispersed them, but a second rising then exploded in Essex, when a vast crowd of men gathered in Great Baddow churchyard and moved down to Norsey Wood to take up battle positions against the King's army. So confident of victory were the peasants that they drew up a line of carts and wagons at the edge of the wood so that their womenfolk might have a grandstand view of their success. But they were no match for the military and, driven back, they were prevented from escaping by the barrier of their own carts. By the end of the day five hundred Essex families had lost their breadwinners. Their sacrifice was not in vain, for the lords from that time on were forced to introduce a system of money payment for labour and a slow improvement in living standards resulted.

Old Cottage, Chapel Street

BLACK NOTLEY

A village due south of Braintree noted today for its large hospital which overlooks the vale of the river Brain. The Hall and the church stand together in green and pleasant isolation. Their history runs from Norman times, as windows in St Peter and St Paul's prove, and is continued in the big barn by the Hall, built all of wood in the 15th century.

On 29th November 1628, the wife of the village blacksmith presented him with a son whom they called John, and John Ray made Black Notley famous. He was fortunate in gaining admission to Cambridge University, where he won recognition as a classical scholar, a theologian and, above all, as a systematic naturalist. One authority places him next to Charles Darwin in importance in this field. He toured the country compiling a comprehensive flora and, with the help of friends, also toured Europe, returning at last to live in his native village where he received letters and parcels of specimens from universities and individuals around the world. In his great work, *The History of Plants* 1686–1704, he put over 11,000 plants into a methodical classification never previously attempted. It is said that he received just £5 for this work, but the respect in which he was held during his lifetime is evinced by the memorial erected in the churchyard, which was paid for by the Bishop of London, no less, and included a long, flowing Latin inscription, of which part may be translated:

'Hid in this narrow tomb, this marble span,
Lies all that death could snatch from this great man;
His body moulders in its native clay,
While o'er wide worlds his works their beams display,
As bright and everlasting as the day.
To those just fame ascribed immortal breath,
And in his writings he outlives his death.'

The pargetted portrait plaque which decorates the house built on the site of Ray's home is one of the many examples throughout the county of the work of a modern pargetter, Fred Willett.

BOCKING

A beautiful view of the place where the former cloth towns of Bocking and Braintree meet epitomises the early importance of these places. 'Bradford Street, Bocking is one of the best medieval streets in East Anglia' says the current county handbook. The old houses interspersed with Georgian and Victorian infilling together constitute a veritable architectural cavalcade, showing how two villages, in which weaving was established back in the 14th century, grew on the profits from the weaving industry into two towns which finally merged as one urban district in 1934.

Bocking's Church of St Mary is all 15th-century building except for the chancel, which is a century older, though its very unusual stained glass with large figures in deep, glowing colours is, surprisingly, mid-Victorian.

Near the church beside the river was built the mill in which Samuel Courtauld founded the fortune of this famous family of weavers when the company he formed began production in 1816. Today a large factory occupies that site, dwarfing the church, and more than 110,000 people all over the country and abroad have Courtauld to thank for their bread and butter.

North-east, at the top of Church Street, stands a post mill, built about 1680, but moved here onto a brick roundhouse in 1830; it is not working now, but can be visited.

BOREHAM 1

'The Princess Mary, afterwards Queen Mary I, was in residence at the palace of New Hall, Boreham, at the time of Elizabeth's birth and at various times afterwards.' So says Sir William Addison in his *Essex Worthies*, and that alone makes the place worthy of further investigation.

The whole estate once belonged to Waltham Abbey, up to about 1351, then it passed through the hands of many owners down to the Botelers who were granted by Henry VII the right to embattle and fortify their manor house. It passed on marriage to Sir William Boleyn, grandfather of that ill-fated Anne who ventured to win a crown and lost her life. So it was that Henry VIII bought New Hall in 1517 and modernised the place to suit his requirements as a royal residence. It is recorded that he held the important Feast of St George there in 1524. Queen Elizabeth granted it to Thomas Radcliffe, Earl of Sussex, whose alabaster effigy, together with those of his father and grandfather, marks his tomb in Boreham church, in 1573. It was sold to George Villiers, Duke of Buckingham, for £30,000 in 1620 and sequestered from that family by the Parliamentarians who allowed Oliver Cromwell to buy it for just five shillings!

BOREHAM 2

Cromwell very soon exchanged New Hall for Hampton Court and finally it reverted to the family at the Restoration to be bought for General Monk by a government grateful for his part in effecting the return of the monarchy, for which he was also created Duke of Albemarle. Until his death in 1669 he lived at New Hall on the grand scale, entertaining the King and many people of note.

At last, in 1737 this great house and its grounds were sold as a separate entity to a rich merchant, John Olmius, who must have viewed the massive, and by now fast decaying, structure with some apprehension. He is said to have demolished nine-tenths of this royal pile, including the chapel whose painted window was originally intended for St Margaret's, Westminster. After two hundred years' existence at Boreham, including burial for protection during the Civil War, it was bought back and installed at last in that church. The great quadrangles of buildings are represented now only by the subterranean drains which spread out so far that legends are rife of tunnels from here to just about everywhere.

The extensive remains of that fabulous Hall now accommodate a girls' school run by the Canonesses of the Holy Sepulchre who came here in 1798. The south facade of the house as we see it today dates from 1573, but it was badly damaged by bombs in 1943 and subsequently restored. Sic transit gloria mundi!

BORLEY

The church has a Norman nave and Elizabethan monuments including the fine Waldegrave tomb. There is no indication there of the furore created in the village when the national press took up the claim that the rectory was haunted. The Reverend A. C. Henning came here in 1936 and saw '... the lovely rolling countryside of Essex where it borders on Suffolk ... Borley stands looking down to the valley of the Stour ... the church is the crowning glory of the hill ...' But he did not wish to live in the dark and dilapidated rectory, built in 1863, '... in view of its gloomy reputation ...' 'for no-one doubts that ... the name of "That Most Haunted House in England" was fully justified ...'

Local legend had it that medieval monk and nun, caught eloping from the monastery on this site were put to death, and are seen gliding about along with ghostly coach and ghastly headless coachman. The rumours excited the Rector to write to the Daily Mirror in June 1929; Harry Price, well-known psychical researcher and journalist was brought in and from then the more violent manifestations occurred. It was all too much for the Rector, he left; the Rectory remained empty for six months, with no hauntings observed, and then when the Foysters came to the living in 1930, spirit writing and poltergeist activity brought renewed world-wide publicity until the Rector's wife came under suspicion, and after an 'exorcism' by local spiritualists, the supernatural activity ceased abruptly. Price himself rented the Rectory for a year in 1937 and the Rector kept vigil there along with 48 'investigators' who claimed various strange happenings, but he could not come to a firm conclusion himself and felt that extraneous stories of witchcraft and Black Mass practised here have clouded the real issue. On 27th February 1939, at midnight, the rectory was burnt down; the remains were sold as rubble to build wartime aerodromes, yet there is still a pilgrimage of the curious, the sensation seekers, to this quiet, country spot. The whole story was summed up in 1956 by Dingwall and others in their *The Haunting of Borley Rectory*.

BRADWELL-JUXTA-MARE 1

Park the car and walk the long straight track to the sea wall, and there
it is, the oldest church in the county and one of the oldest in the whole
country; for this is the church built to the orders of St Cedd around 654,
when he came ashore to persuade the Saxons of the true religion.

It is such a simple building, now nothing but a nave; although it has
been confirmed that it had a chancel in the shape of an apse and a porch
at the west end. St Cedd's landfall was propitious. He found here the
remains of Othona, one of the Roman Forts of the Saxon Shore with walls
12ft thick and about 500ft long. Much of it, then and since, has been
swallowed by the sea. St Cedd was able to dismantle the 400-year-old
ruins and use brick and stone to build St Peter-on-the-Wall astride the
western wall of Othona. The stark simplicity of this 1300-year-old
church, outlined against a background of sea and sky evokes respect for
the determination of those early Christians, and demonstrates that their
confidence in their faith was fully justified. But for many years the
church's true purpose was lost and it was used as a barn. Through the
generosity of an unknown man it was repaired and re-consecrated on
22nd June 1920 and each year the Bishop of Chelmsford leads a
pilgrimage to this ancient holy place.

BRADWELL-JUXTA-MARE 2

Standing in the shadow of the church of St Thomas the Apostle is a building which could not contrast more with that place of piety and prayer. It is the village 'cage', a small building of brick under a tiled roof with a stout wooden door to prevent the escape of those village miscreants the constable had to incarcerate until they could be taken to the nearest town and brought before the court.

Although it was erected in 1817 by local builder Samuel Horne it was firmly enough built to last for more than one hundred and fifty years so far, and though that builder did not have the advantage of a technical college training he still showed his own originality in setting bricks at an angle to add a little decoration just under the eaves; and the whole thing cost just £3.10s.9d . Beside the door can be seen the remains of the pillory where hands would be imprisoned when a lawbreaker was to be whipped; entertainment and example, laid on by the birch.

The church itself has work in nave and chancel which indicates 14th-century origins, with a brick tower of 1706, while the cottages, gabled and plastered, give the village green a nostalgic picturesqueness.

BRAINTREE 1

The Horn Inn: This ancient hostelry is only one of very many inns which once lined the streets of Braintree all the way down to Bradford Street where wide, old gateways indicate the sites of those long since demolished, rebuilt or adapted as private houses. The reason for such a large number is attributed to Braintree's key position on the pilgrim routes of pre-Reformation times, when travelling for pilgrim, chapman, or just plain everyman, was slow and tedious. Inns offered rest, food, drink and social intercourse, and their signs made their purpose evident to the illiterate.

The White Hart survives as a timber and plaster building facing the flood of traffic round the one-way system into Bank Street. It was built in the 17th century with alterations in the following century. Further down, the Swan Inn is contemporary, with a rambling facade including exposed timbers. The Horn, built in the 18th century, has all the appearance, and rightly so, of a coaching inn with bay windows pushing out onto the pavement either side of the wide archway, through to what were the stables. Its appearance today is very much as it can be seen in the well-known print of Braintree market in 1808.

BRAINTREE 2

This old town does not rely solely on ancient architecture for its good looks. Beside the High Street where it meets St Michael's Road can be seen a fountain. A young boy in bronze, standing high on a plinth in the centre of a pool holds a shell in one hand and a fish in the other. From them, and from the mouths of animals at the pool's edge, issue forth the jets of water which make a refreshing sight and sound, a really pleasant feature with which to draw attention to the nearby parish church of St Michael. The fountain, designed by John Hodge, was installed about 1938.

Another fountain, intended to slake the thirst rather than improve the scenery was built much earlier, in 1882, to the order of George Courtauld, in Market Square and presented to the town; just one of the many bequests to Braintree and Bocking by that famous weaving family. In fact the very Town Hall which keeps the fountain company was completed in 1928 and presented to the town by Mr W. J. Courtauld. It was designed by Vincent Harris as a neat, two-storeyed building under an open bell turret crowned with a cupola and topped by a bronze figure representing truth. The walls within have been splendidly decorated with murals by Maurice Grieffenhagen and the ceilings are decorated by Henry Rushbury.

BRAINTREE 3

Braintree's origin goes back to an unusual prehistoric lake settlement, proved by pottery and other finds in the area. In later days the town was governed by the self-perpetuating 'Company of Four and Twenty' — important inhabitants who carefully kept power in their hands. But this was not acceptable to 18th-century standards of government and open elections were introduced. In 1934 Braintree and Bocking were merged as one Urban District and continued until 1974 when they became the centre of a new District. Whilst the Courtaulds contributed greatly to Braintree's prosperity, another great benefactor was Francis Crittall, simply through the employment he has provided for thousands since he developed his father's ironmongery into a factory for making metal windows in about 1886 and so established a company which has achieved international status. The factory is a landmark in Braintree life as well as in its landscape. An interesting demonstration of Crittall's attitude to his workmen is that he was the first employer to introduce a five-day working week. He even built, nearby, a factory specially designed to employ the disabled. That was in 1926. At the same time he realised his dream of a special village for his workpeople in the building of Silver End, where they could live and work in the healthiest possible environment.

Silver End —
Memorial Gardens　29

A simple granite obelisk on the pavement by the busy High Street takes the reader of its inscription back four hundred years. On one side it says, 'To the pious memory of William Hunter, a native of Brentwood who, maintaining his right to search the scriptures, and in all matters of faith and practice to follow their sole guidance, was condemned at the early age of nineteen, by Bishop Bonner in the reign of Queen Mary and burned at the stake near this spot March XXVI, MDLV.'

Having been seen in the chapel-of-ease, which Brentwood enjoyed as a hamlet of South Weald, reading the Bible for himself, and questioned as to his beliefs, William could not express agreement to the belief that the bread and wine of the Sacrament were the true flesh and blood of Christ. He was reported upwards from Justice Anthony Browne, founder of the Grammar School, to Bishop Bonner in London, who tried to get the young man to conform, but William's knowledge of the scriptures and his unshakable conviction resisted threats and bribes and so he was brought back to his home town to be burnt as an example to other protestants.

The obelisk was put up in 1861. In 1907 a severe fire, which burnt down the shop on the corner beside it, so cracked and damaged the granite that it had to be repaired. It was restored by September 1910, as recorded on it.

BRENTWOOD 2

Old House is more than ancient bricks and mortar. Doris Stump, author of its printed history, writes: 'It can be seen that throughout the years Old House has always served a useful purpose. Its history is interesting and its use today as an Arts and Community Centre is very much in demand.' Though it has been established that a house has existed on this site since 1748 the builder and the owner cannot be traced. Through the years it served for a time as the Red Lion inn and then as a family home on the edge of town with a garden all about it. Under the ownership of Isaac Rist in 1888, when he was a grocer in the High Street it was joined with the house next door. It seems that even then it had that luxuriant Virginia Creeper which so attractively clothes its walls today.

In 1918 it was leased from the Rists by Brentwood School, and then in 1930 headmaster James Hough bought it outright to present to the school. During the Second World War it served as an outpost of the London Hospital, then, in 1966, the School sold it to the Post Office who used it until 1971. Brentwood Council then decided to buy it and adapt it to the functions of an Arts Centre which was opened in 1973. Now it is an acknowledged and popular centre for literary, musical and artistic activity over a wide area around Brentwood.

BRENTWOOD 3

It may have been Sir Anthony Browne's regret at his enforced involvement
in the examination and burning of martyr William Hunter which caused
him to reflect on the need for education and enlightenment in the parish
of which he was the squire. In October 1557 he bought the land on which
School House and the Old School stand today. The school received its
charter from Queen Mary on 5th July 1558 and George Otway became
the first headmaster. Browne was knighted by Queen Elizabeth and
appointed Chief Justice of the Court of Common Pleas before his death
in 1567, when his will concerning '... the Grammar School of Anthony
Browne, Serjeant at Law, in Brentwood ...' was proved. The following
year the present Old School was built as shown by the foundation stone
over the doorway dated 10th April 1568. It was an oversight that
Browne's statutes for the conduct of the school were not made legal,
so they had to be redrawn in 1622 by trustees who included the poet
John Donne.

Rules included '... in the summer tyme to begin at sixe of the clocke
in the morneinge and to leave at sixe of the clocke at night ...' — a long
school day! Local boys were admitted free. Over the last century the
school has expanded and advanced out of all recognition, educating over
a thousand pupils of whom nearly a quarter are boarders.

BRENTWOOD 4

The remains of the 13th-century chapel built by David, Abbot of St Osyth, which stand in the High Street next to the Odeon cinema are slight indeed, but in their time they have been the stage for two dramas of history.

In 1232 Henry III accused his former regent, Hubert de Burgh, of malfeasance during his minority. As Hubert was on his way to London to answer the charges, soldiers directed by the Steward of the Royal Household sought him out at Brentwood, where he just had time to race from his bed to sanctuary in the chapel of St Thomas, facing his pursuers with the host in one hand and the cross in the other. The soldiers defied the sanctuary, dragged Hubert out and ordered the local blacksmith to prepare fetters. This man's refusal to obey them because of his admiration for the great man's service to the country has become a legend, but that did not stop Hubert's removal to the Tower of London. The Bishop of London was affronted; he threatened to excommunicate all concerned, so the King was forced to return Hubert to his sanctuary in the chapel, but he knew that such sanctuary could continue for forty days only, so he had his soldiers sit out the period in a siege of the chapel so that they could once again take their man. The outcome was happy — a loss of certain grants and an unharrassed retirement.

It was Wistan Browne, nephew and heir to Sir Anthony, who claimed the chapel as his property and began to pull it down systematically. This angered the local people so much that on 5th August 1577 a great crowd of women gathered in the chapel and shut the doors on Browne's men. They had collected together an armoury of strange weapons — hot spits, one bow and nine arrows, two kettles of hot water and a great sharp stone among them, to discourage entry and prevent further demolition.

The law intervened, the Privy Council, no less, ordered the women to be freed on bail, halted the demolition and asked Browne to explain himself. The Chapel was eventually declared to be the property of the townsfolk and that Tudor 'sit-in' by determined women showed what can be achieved by concerted action.

BRIGHTLINGSEA

You come upon All Saints church before you reach the present outskirts of this little seaside town. Its strong, bold tower is a landmark rising from the trees. A rounded arch in the wall of the south aisle incorporates Roman brick and points to the church's erection in early Norman times, though much of what we see now is of the Perpendicular period (1335–1530) when this part of the county was a prosperous cloth-producing area. There are many features to catch the eye, including fine old brasses to members of the Beriffe family ranging from 1496 to 1578 in the North Chapel.

At the other extreme of taste in memorial art is the sumptuous monument to Nicholas Magens who died in 1764. He was a German who made a mint of money in the London insurance business. His monument was erected in the chancel in 1779, and features our globe with an angel beside it holding a parchment scroll with the inscription, while cherubs peep from clouds above and an anchor, ships and a cornucopia complete the symbolism of the man's achievement, though of his likeness there is none.

More touching in their utter simplicity are the tiles, placed in a continuous line around the nave, each one of which is inscribed to the memory of a parishioner who died at sea. They were begun in 1872 by the Revd Arthur Pertwee and continued through the legacy of William Stammers, one-time churchwarden.

BURNHAM-ON-CROUCH 1

The main street has yielded precedence to the quayside, but this is not surprising for this town is the largest yachting centre on the east coast, though it means that the church of St Mary stands a mile north of the present town. So many older people have retired here that the local wag assured me: 'They all come into Burnham down the B1010 (the only road into the town) and go out of it through the church door.' From that church the road runs south, with houses gathering the more thickly till it comes to the quay and veers east to open out into one of the county's broadest high streets, where the Carnival and fair have long been an annual event enjoyed by landsmen and yachtsmen alike, in the shadow of the Clock Tower which bestrides the pavement. Though it wears all the authority of the Town Hall clock it is, in fact, an added embellishment of the endowed schools, made in memory of Laban Sweeting in 1877. The schools, administered by the Burnham Charity Trust, had already been enlarged in 1863. Now they have a neglected air as they await the development which has already provided car parking, seats and landscaping on the other side of the road.

'Burnham is on the banks of the River Crouch, which is here about three-quarters of a mile in width, has water enough for large ships and is navigable for ten miles above the town for vessels of 300 tons ...' Thus the County Directory of 1937 gets to the heart of the town's attraction — water, and those things which bob about on it called boats. 'The Cowes of the East Coast' starts for sailors at Shore Road and the beginning of the quay, 'the essence and spirit of Burnham on Crouch'.

Anybody can walk the length of the quay and see boatyards, hotels, homes and gardens to port — and to starboard, boats, boats and more boats reaching away to the east where the white bulk of the Royal Corinthian Yacht Club, built in 1931, appears in the heat haze to be a shimmering ghost ship itself. To the west the quay peters out in a path which runs riverside to Creeksea.

During Burnham's Yachting Week there can be more than 3,000 boats on the river, which was secured by the Crouch River Harbour Authority in 1978 for £80,000 from the company which had acquired the river, oyster beds and breeding equipment once vested in the Lords of Burnham Manor. The Harbour Authority has thereby saved the river from commercial exploitation for sand and gravel. Yachtsmen should be grateful!

CANVEY ISLAND

There will still be a good many people who remember crossing the creek at low tide on the stepping stones which connected Canvey Island with the outside world, in the form of Benfleet's grassy slope. Such a primitive state of affairs was remedied by the building of a £20,000 bridge in 1931. Long before this development the six-mile long, three-mile wide island had, for hundreds of years, only been used for summer grazing because of its constant inundation.

A syndicate of business men saw the advantages of embanking the whole island and secured the engineer Cornelius Vermuyden together with an army of Dutchmen who completed the work by 1623. Apart from the appearance of some very unusual names at local baptisms the only reminders of that vital period in the island's story are the sea walls themselves and a couple of cottages, both known as the Dutch Cottage, eight-sided and thatch-roofed. The one in Haven Road was built in 1621, the other, three years older, was given to the Council in 1952. They had it carefully repaired and opened it ten years later as the Canvey Island Dutch Cottage Museum. It is kept open every summer weekend by local Historical Society members. A collection has been formed typical of the cottage and its times, including a barrow and the tools used to build that embankment.

CASTLE HEDINGHAM 1

If it had not have been for Aubrey de Vere there would not have been a
village of this name for, though Hedingham was the settlement of a Saxon
tribe, the Castle was created by that Norman lord who was rewarded
for his loyalty to William the Conqueror with this and thirteen other
Essex manors, understandably so when we hear that he married William's
sister! He arranged to have the castle built in about 1140 with the bold,
square keep of Barnack stone on its mount rising way above the old trees
around it. The two surviving corner-turrets bring its total height to just
about 100ft. It has been described by an expert as '... probably the best
preserved of all tower-keeps of England'. The mound on which it stands
is called the Inner Bailey; the Outer Bailey can be recognised still where
it runs round the house, of Georgian origin, which is a private residence.

The keep's interior suffered from a fire in recent years, but the walls,
12ft thick at the base, would probably survive an earthquake, and there
are many features to be enjoyed, like the great arch which spans the first
floor and the 800-year-old fireplace beneath Norman zig-zag decoration.
The beautiful brick bridge over the moat dates from the beginning of the
16th century.

CASTLE HEDINGHAM 2

Anyone who takes a stroll along the village street will agree with the former Halstead Rural District Council: 'Below the Castle and around the Church are the red-brick and timber houses of the village itself, unspoilt and delightful even in this highly commercial age.' The centre of the village is the triangle formed by Bayley, St James and Crown Streets, where the Old Falcon and the Wheatsheaf show Tudor timber work. Their beams surely echoed the discussion which preceded the rebuilding of the church tower in 1616. The battlements which top St Nicholas' Norman walls are of that same Tudor brick, and so is the clerestory. Inside there is something of every period to demonstrate that it is the outward sign of the spiritual life of a village through nearly a thousand years.

The unique churchyard cross combining Saxon and Norman elements was found in the cellar of the Falcon between the wars and set up as a monument to The Fallen. The church's great feature is the marvellous 'double hammerbeam' roof of 16th-century craftsmanship above the splendidly carved capitals of the pillars of the nave arcade which has been dated to around 1180. In the chancel can be seen these 'misericords' which, by humorously carved rests on the base of the hinged seats, allowed the long-standing worshipper a kind of prop.

The beautiful brick bridge over the moat — 16th Century

CHAPPEL

Chappel's church beneath its pointed spire is a simple place of prayer some six hundred years old; the other 'skyscraper' of that ancient village was the mill, seen now as a three-storied weatherboarded building of the 18th century. A very old right of way goes through the centre of the village where St Barnabas's and a row of attractive houses form a backdrop for the little green. A more intriguing view is offered further on where the path approaches the quarter-of-a-mile long viaduct. The great supporting columns are pierced with holes through which vignettes of the river valley are glimpsed. It was the viaduct and the railway it carried which changed the country way of life when it was completed in 1849. Strangely enough there are thirty two arches each of nearly 32ft span; it is 320yds long and it cost £32,000. At one time it carried trains from Cambridge to Clacton as well as all the business of the Stour Valley and Colne Valley railways. The viaduct is now classified as an ancient monument and rightly so, for it was the largest viaduct on the Great Eastern Railway and is still the largest of any kind in East Anglia. At 75ft high its bulk and its weight are enormous, it is estimated that 7,000,000 bricks went into it, yet it looks gracefully light in the landscape.

CHELMSFORD 1

The county town has moved into the 20th century determined to keep up-to-date; so much of its atmosphere has been lost in rebuilding of shops and offices and re-alignment of roads. But one building keeps its place in the town square as it has done since 1791. It is the Shire Hall, a pleasantly square-looking place put up to the design of John Johnson, the county surveyor. It should be recorded that under his personal supervision the work was completed within the time stipulated and the cost estimated so satisfactorily that at the first Quarter Sessions held in the court room in 1792, he was presented by the county with a valuable silver cup. The 96ft by 80ft block contains courts which have been redesigned in recent times and a very handsome, original upper room running the length of the building which has seen very important people present at some of the grandest county functions.

From the street a notable feature of the Ionic-columned facade is the positioning, high up, of three deeply carved plaques representing the human embodiment of the qualities of Wisdom, Justice and Mercy, three moderating influences in the conduct of the courts within. The clock on the pediment was put up in 1887 to mark Queen Victoria's Golden Jubilee, presented by local bankers Sparrow and Company.

Bewigged and thoughtful in his seat of justice, with a hand resting on one of the many tomes of law he contributed to as Chief Justice of the Court of Common Pleas, Sir Nicholas Conyngham Tindal, in effigy, looks from his plinth in the middle of Tindal Square across to the Shire Hall, the county seat of justice. Grandson of the well-known priest and historian of the same name, Tindal was born in 1776 to the wife of a Chelmsford solicitor at Coval Hall, a site in Moulsham Street marked by a plaque. From Chelmsford Grammar School he went to Cambridge, studied law, and was eventually elected to the House of Commons. But it was as a lawyer that he was most successful and by 1829, as Lord Chief Justice, he had reached the peak of his profession. His obituary in *The Times* extolled his legal ability: '... he dissipated the obscurities, lopped off the irrelevancies ... which had been imported into the cause by the weak and evil advocate.'

The statue, by Baily, was paid for by public subscription and erected in 1847, a year after Tindal's death. Bronze lions' heads at the base on two sides of the plinth show that water once poured into horsetroughs set beside it — the remnant of the town's first official water supply.

CHELMSFORD 3

The stone bridge at the foot of Chelmsford's High Street restricted traffic flow so much that a one-way system and a ring road were introduced. Thus the bridge has ensured its own preservation! Though the town gives its name to the river Chelmer it is in fact the Can which divides the town from its Moulsham suburb. It is surmised that the Romans bridged it successfully in the 1st century, but by Saxon times the bridge had disappeared and Coelmer's ford was the crossing place. The Norman Bishop of London, Maurice, saw the opportunities for trade in this, his Manor, if the rivers were bridged. He set this in hand around 1100 and thus made Chelmsford a centre of communication in the county and so, ultimately, county town.

His bridge was replaced by a more substantial stone bridge in 1372, designed by that same Henry of Yvele who was responsible for the nave of Westminster Abbey. But even his bridge could not cope with the ever increasing volume and weight of traffic after four hundred years of continuous use. In 1787 it was completely rebuilt in the form in which we see it today. Its architect, John Johnson, county surveyor 1792–1812, used for the balusters an artificial stone called Coadestone of which the recipe is said to be lost.

CHELMSFORD 4

The unusual facade of the Abbey National offices makes it obvious that it has housed some business other than a modern building society. Old directories show that it was, in Victorian times, the headquarters of the *Essex Chronicle* and its associated newspapers, with titles changing down the years. That makes it a very important place indeed in the Chelmsford story, for surely it is the local newspaper which tells the local story and keeps green the halting memory.

This newspaper first came off the press in August 1764, the twelfth oldest paper in the whole country, and it has recorded local news every week since then with but one break through a strike in 1975 when one edition did not appear. From the old printing shop upstairs where linotype machines made the rafters tremble, the business was removed to new premises on the Westway in 1964 where papers and magazines are produced at high speed by computer-composing and web-offset printing.

It has been suggested that the two portrait busts on the facade of the old office in town represent the physiognomy of the owners of the time, Meggy and Chalk.

Before Judge Tindal's statue edged it out of the central spot in the town square, the fountainhead, or conduit, took pride of place. Until the extension and improvement of the town's water supply in Victorian times this was the only public place where water might be had. Its original establishment is lost in history, but the possibility is that the Black Friars introduced the scheme when they came to the town in the 13th century. There was a strong-flowing stream from a well in a field near the town centre, remembered in the street called Burgesswell Road. It was arched over with bricks so that its flow was forced through wooden water pipes, cleverly jointed, down to that central square where it issued from the 'conduit'. At first this was a simple affair, then it was embellished and crowned with a life-size figure of a naiad in 1792 to match the magnificence of the new Shire Hall overlooking it. But the figure, though fine, somehow reduced the flow of water, so it was replaced in 1814 by a 'rotundiform' structure as illustrated, from which the water continued to flow down the main street and into the river. When the Tindal statue was put up in 1847 this fountainhead was moved to the High Street — Springfield Road junction where it stayed until 1940, redundant but decorative, and an increasing hazard to the growing flow of traffic. So it was moved on again to its present position in Tower Gardens where it crowns a grassy knoll. Unfortunately it stands as dry as it is high, but the inscription engraved upon it in Latin, back in 1814, can still be read and translated:

> 'Bountiful to the bounteous:
> Liberal to the covetous:
> Not diminished by bestowing.
> Such is Divine charity, from the fount of heaven.'

CHELMSFORD 6

Early in 1978 Chelmsford prison suffered severely from a fire which raged through the central block — a sad way to celebrate its 150th anniversary! When it was built in 1828 it was hailed as the very latest in design and in the treatment of prisoners. Previously the gaol stood down by the river, on the Moulsham side, but conditions were so bad that prisoners still awaiting trial, and possibly innocent, died of disease before their cases could be heard.

The new prison, as described in 1831, had new ways: 'The discipline of this prison operates in a salutary manner on the minds of the prisoners. They are prevented from that intercourse in the day-rooms and sleeping-wards, so calculated to spread moral contagion among the inmates of a prison; if they are not made better by coercion at least they are not made worse by contamination. The very cleanliness to which they are subject, is no small part of the punishment ...' Such ideas are outdated, but they were then as advanced as the treadmills which prisoners walked to grind flour and so earn their keep. Though the internal routine of the prison has totally changed its external appearance is very much the same, just as forbidding behind its high walls.

CHIGWELL 1

It was Dickens who put it so neatly: 'Chigwell, my dear fellow, is the
greatest place in the world ... Such a delicious old inn opposite the
churchyard — such a lovely ride — such beautiful forest scenery — such
an out-of-the-way rural place ...' The inn was, and still is, the King's Head,
which Dickens borrowed for Barnaby Rudge, calling it 'The Maypole'.
As it stands today it shows the sympathetic enlargement of 1901 in the
same half-timbered style. It was first built in the 17th century and still
shows some original timbers and decorative work. Its gables and bay
windows, its casements and the timber and plaster contrast of black
and white, added to its setting on the hillside opposite the church amidst
its trees, all make a very picturesque view.

The church of St Mary, originally Norman and rebuilt in the 15th
century to serve a village congregation, was enlarged in 1886 to more than
twice its size to accommodate the growing population, though the place
has made great efforts to retain its individuality as the first village out
of London on the A113.

CHIGWELL 2

The chancel of St Mary's was resited and refurbished in 1886; on its wall
was mounted the ancient brass which once marked the burial place of
Samuel Harsnett, Archbishop of York. This is a famous monument for it
is the latest known example of a brass to a bishop, showing an image
almost life-size fully dressed in cope, alb, dalmatic and stole. Around
the edge, the arbishop's own words are inscribed in Latin which can be
translated: 'Here lies Samuel Harsnett, formerly vicar of this church
and afterwards, first, the unworthy bishop of Chichester, then the more
unworthy bishop of Norwich and, lastly, the very unworthy archbishop
of York,' He died 25th May 1631, having asked that he should be buried
in the parish where he first practised his priesthood from 1597 to 1605.
His obvious affection for Chigwell led him to found the Grammar School
here in 1629, for which he drew up careful conditions. For example, the
Latin master was to be 'no puffer of tobacco' and the scholar who swore
was to feel the rod, but no more than three strokes at any one time. That
first school-room survives as the centre of the modern public school
which has expanded far beyond the dreams of its founder, whose bust
reminds today's scholars of the ancient roots of their enlightened
education.

CHIPPING ONGAR

This ancient town on the west bank of the river Roding and east of the Cripsey brook has been brought slap-bang into the 20th century as the last stop on London Underground's Central Line. It is a 'one-street' town, where the variety of architecture represents pages in its story through the ages, for the greater part of which it was altogether within the confines of the entrenchments of a great Norman castle built in 1162 by Richard de Lucy and demolished in the days of the first Elizabeth, in favour of a big Tudor house which has itself been reduced to dust.

The Congregational church, founded in 1690 and rebuilt in 1833, is as well-known as the parish church of St Martin, built seven hundred years earlier, because it has a memorial to the Revd Isaac Taylor, a former minister, and to his daughter Jane, who died in 1824. Her fame went round the world as the author, with her sister Ann, of 'Original Poems for Infant Minds ...' which included 'Twinkle, twinkle little star ...' It is almost by the way that, close at hand, David Livingstone (1813–1873) the celebrated explorer and missionary, had a room for two years in the course of his training for the ministry.

CLACTON

Clacton has been the butt of many a small-time comedian's jokes about the English at the seaside. If they gave themselves the pleasure of visiting the place they would afford it greater respect. The spirit of Clacton is captured, and dispensed, at its pier. It was built in 1873, all of timber, and just before the last war it was widened and extended to 1150ft on piles of reinforced concrete. Time was when the pleasure steamers from Southend called here in a creaming of white water and a streaming of black smoke. Now they are out of fashion and the pier, which could then seat a thousand people in its pavilion has changed its attractions to dance hall, sun deck, swimming pool, amusement halls and a theatre seating 1275 people.

On Ascension Day 1882 the first train puffed into the clapboard station, and Clacton had arrived! Holiday-makers and trippers have continued to come in large numbers, making their way to the pier and its pastimes. In 1904 that pier and its crowding promenaders saw the amazing sight on a summer's day of 150,000 troops wading ashore from landing craft in mock-invasion manoeuvres. At the end of a day of attack on, and retreat from, Colchester the soldiers re-embarked to the applause of holiday-makers who crowded round the observing members of the General Staff.

COGGESHALL

This was a town of no little importance in the days when the making of cloth put gold in Essex men's pockets. Coggeshall has its own special reputation for lace-making, practised into this century and the subject of a recent book. More recently it has gained a reputation as the centre of a seed-growing area.

Its big old church was badly damaged in the last war, but that can hardly be believed today, for its ruined nave and battlemented west tower were completely rebuilt as they had been in the 15th century. In the north chapel can be seen brasses to the Paycocke family, including Thomas, buried in 1580. They bring recollection of those days of cloth and prosperity, for this was a family of wool merchants who had a splendid house built at the beginning of the 16th century, when John Paycocke, dying in 1505, left to his son Thomas, 'My house ... in the West Street of Coggeshall, afore the Vicarage ...' By 1584 the family had died out but the house carried on, to be described as it stands today as: 'One of the most attractive half-timbered houses of England, regardless of the fact that much of its facade is restored.' It is fortunate that it is now in the care of the National Trust, and open to the public on mid-week summer afternoons.

COLCHESTER 1

'Old King Cole was a merry old soul' — says the jingle and it is nice to imagine that he did infuse a little jollity into the ancient Colchester scene, for there are a number of local features which bear his name. The Ancient British entrenchments at Lexden are called King Cole's Kitchen and the site of the Castle itself was known by natives of an earlier age as King Cole's Palace. This latter was a most important site — the forum, the market place and the law courts of the great Roman colony at Camulodunum. Under the Castle keep are the remains of the Temple which Tacitus recorded as being built in honour of Claudius who led the great Roman invasion of this headquarters of the British tribes in 43 AD.

Just as the Romans built impressively to dominate the British, so the Normans demonstrated their superiority over the Anglo-Saxons in the building of mighty castles. Eudo, William's 'dapifer' or steward of his Normandy possessions, was rewarded for his loyalty after the great invasion with Colchester and many other manors. It may have been the severe Danish raid in 1071, when the town was burnt down, that determined Eudo to build his great castle by 1076. The area of its pallisaded enclosure was bigger even than the Tower of London. Most impressive was the great keep which never had to resist an enemy other than in civil war when in 1216, the Barons' force was besieged here after the granting of Magna Carta. It was reduced in that century to the status of a prison, continuing as such down to 1840.

Sometime in the 17th century it was sold by its owners, the Norfolk family, to John Wheely, an ironmonger in the town, on condition that he demolished it. He tried, but the Norman masons had been too thorough, Wheely just had to give up. So it passed into more sensitive hands and its preservation was assured when Lord Cowdray and his wife bought it and presented it to the Borough in 1920, 'as an evidence of their affection for Colchester and in memory of the men who so nobly fought and suffered in the War.'

Now it houses a museum known internationally for its Romano-British collection, the largest assembled from a single site, with many valuable and some unique objects. It is called in constantly to fresh discoveries such as the large bronze image of Mercury found at Gosbeck's Farm, Shrub End in 1947, which has been dated to 150 AD.

COLCHESTER 2

The Romans had been in Camulodunum, which they wrested from the British King Cunobelin in 43 AD, for just a century when they set in hand the building of a mighty wall to protect their increasingly important headquarters and their growing colony. Gateways were arched over and made defensible. But the town's importance in modern times brought such a burden of traffic that these old gates were doomed when roads were widened, and the walls were robbed of their valuable building stone almost from the day the Romans left around 407.

So there is only a mile-and-a-half of that wall left, best seen on Balkerne Hill. At its summit will be seen the only gateway left to modern sight. Its very name indicates the reason for its survival. In Saxon days the Danes had the nasty habit of sailing up the Colne and catching the burgesses unawares, so they blocked up this, the main gateway, on the western side, to improve their defences, and 'balk' access. Since it was no longer used and the road was diverted, there was no need to demolish it in later days! The remains of this gateway may look insignificant beside today's sky-scrapers, but it ranks as one of the largest in Roman Britain, with four arches — two for vehicles and two for pedestrians. A public house was built on the remains of one of the watchtowers and across the roadway. Once called the King's Head it is now known as The Hole in the Wall — its name since 1961.

COLCHESTER 3

From the bottom of the High Street hill, houses, churches and shops
rise up on either hand in such a mixture of periods and styles that any
view of its development historically is quite confounded. The oldest
building is probably All Saints church, now put to interesting use as a
natural history museum, but a close runner-up is the Red Lion with its
15th-century timbers supporting a projecting upper storey. The George
is also very old, but its front is 18th-century. Rising above all this
ancient and modern architecture is the Town Hall with its Victoria Tower
which was built over the four years to 1901 by Sir John Belcher. It is
unusual and pleasing to read: 'Visitors admitted and shown over the
building free of charge.' It replaced a hall built in 1844 on the same site
as the Norman Moot Hall. The height of the slim, red-brick, stone-crowned
tower is 162ft to the tip of the cross held by the bronze figure of St
Helena, patron saint of Colchester. She is said to have been the daughter
of that King Cole who led a revolt against Roman tyranny. Other
Colchester notables represented by figures on the High Street facade are
Eudo, who built St John's Abbey and was made Lord of Colchester by
William II; Thomas, Lord Audley, Colchester's Town Clerk in 1516, and
later Chancellor under Henry VIII; Dr William Gilberd, native of the
town and physician to Elizabeth I but best known as a pioneer of
electrical science, who died in 1604; and Samuel Harsnett, local boy who
made good to the extent of being appointed Archbishop of York in 1628.
On the Stockwell Street face Boadicea and Edward the Elder are
represented.

COLCHESTER 4

What building is more evocative of those desperate days of the terrible siege of Colchester than the Siege House in East Street? It was built a hundred and fifty years or so before that, on an L-shaped plan, just east of the bridge over the Colne. Its timber work in its projecting upper storey, crowned by big chimney shafts, is a photographer's delight. It had for long been the offices of a local miller's business which was taken over by a national company, but though its future as business premises may be uncertain its preservation as a 'classified' building is assured. Those old timbers front and side are pock-marked by the bullets which flew in that siege in 1648 which lasted from 13th June to 28th August.

Though it has been necessary to restore much of the exterior there are several contemporary features within, like the moulded ceiling beams. In one window can be seen two medallions of stained glass, one dated 1546 quarters the arms of Katherine Parr. They came, it is said, from some other old, unidentified house in the town.

For all its importance in giving its name to the settlement of Colchester, the river which runs beside the Siege House, the Colne, has a simple enough meaning. According to the expert it means — 'water', or 'river'!

From the busy-ness of a main street one comes quite suddenly on the peaceful ruin of St Botolph's Priory church. It is impressive in size and bulk now, yet only the crumbling pillars and walls remain of the west front and the 36yd long nave. The east end and transepts of this imposing church have disappeared long since.

This was the church of the first house of Augustinian Canons to be founded in this country, towards the end of the 11th century, under Norman patronage. It was given a huge, circular west window, the first of its size and type in England. The mighty pillars are nearly 6ft in diameter, and incorporate Roman bricks, which glow in warm red bands against the buff stone and the smooth green grass.

St Botolph's was doomed in the first place by Henry VIII's closure of the Priory at the Reformation, but it was ruined in that twelve-week siege of 1648 when cannon-balls brought it all tumbling down. In the 19th century its floor was used as a burial ground and some tombstones remained after it was taken over by the government as a public monument in 1912.

COLCHESTER 6

Colchester can show tons of Romano–British remains and a number of
Norman buildings, but there is only one part of a building in the town
which represents the period in between, that half a millenium of Saxon
occupation. It is the tower of the Church of the Holy Trinity, just off
Trinity Street. The Saxons robbed Roman ruins of their bricks and gave
the tower a square, clean, deceptively modern look, further encouraged
by the flat pyramid of a roof put up in more recent times. The church
itself was thoroughly restored in 1886, but early features were retained,
including monuments to two famous men: William Gilberd, whose house,
Tymperleys, opposite, bears a memorial plaque; and John Wilbye, the
Elizabethan composer of madrigals, who was buried in the churchyard.
Gilberd lived from 1544 to 1603. His work on electro-magnetism, as
published in *De Magnete* laid the foundations for the study of the subject
in this country.

After a period of neglect, and following much local public pressure
this redundant church was taken over and adapted by the Borough to the
functions of a museum of social history.

Doorway, Church of the Holy Trinity

COPFORD

Where is Copford? Some folk would say it lines the old A12, now re-classified as the B1408 and, thankfully, bypassed; others would have it at Copford Green a mile to the south; and yet another faction would place that ancient 'Coppa's ford' of the Roman River east again beyond those twins of the Saxon settlement, the Church and the Hall. In this wide spreading parish the chief point of interest must be the church of St Mary the Virgin, reckoned to be the most remarkable parish church in the county.

Remote it may be, worth looking for it certainly is, for two good reasons. First, the architecture, a simple 12th-century building of nave, chancel and apse has survived entire, with only the addition of a south aisle sometime in the 14th century and the bell-turret perhaps a century later; the one sad note is that the stone vaulting of the nave and chancel was replaced by timber. Second, the wall paintings. Incredibly, they are contemporary with the building of the church, though they were restored a century ago and again more recently. On the vault of the apse Christ sits in glory, supported by angels, and on nave and chancel walls paintings which illustrated the story of Christianity for illiterate peasants can still be admired, though not always recognised.

CRESSING

Water cress has made a refreshing contribution to our diet since time immemorial, as proved by the name of one Essex village — Cressing, 'the place where cress grows'. It is not a village known to tourists, yet it has a claim to considerable fame through its two barns which stand beside the B1018 more than a mile from the church of All Saints, a 12th-century re-founding by Queen Matilda. The right to appoint its priest was vested very early on in the Knights Templar whose commandery was established here in the same century and naturally came to be called Cressing Temple, though in fact it passed to the Knights Hospitallers of St John of Jerusalem and then, at the dissolution, to the crown.

The barns were thought to have been put up in the 15th century, but radio-carbon dating and new expert opinion puts the construction of the Barley Barn, incredibly, contemporary with the Order's arrival around 1130 and the Wheat Barn a hundred years later. Since there is no stone in Essex, the barns were built entirely of wood — a construction which must be seen from the interior to be appreciated. In the fretwork of timbers supporting the roofs over the 50yd-long barns the beams look deceptively delicate. A third barn, dated 1623 and white-washed keeps them company along with the farmhouse and its moat. A glorious view, but a private one. The barns can be viewed only by appointment.

DAGENHAM

Yes, it is the home of Ford's, and the former village has prospered through it, but at the expense of its homogeneity and its old buildings. But there is still an island of antiquity where the church, mostly of an 1800 re-building, the vicarage and the Cross Keys inn of 15th-century origin stand together. No doubt the Ford factory itself will one day be viewed as an historical monument to the age of petrol. It can, after all, be said to be standing on an historic site.

On 17th December 1707 an extra high tide running up the Thames broke through a sluice gate at this point. Nobody felt it was their responsibility. Tide followed tide and the flood wall went down before them. The breach widened to 100yds and 20ft deep. Thousands of acres were inundated and silt brought out on the ebb formed a great sandbank in the Thames which threatened to stop all shipping. So it became a national crisis and Parliament had to vote a special tax on Thames traffic to finance the repair. One, William Boswell, offered to effect it for £16,500, but when all that money was spent the water still lapped at Dagenham's door. It was not until 1715 that Captain Perry came forward to attempt a solution. It took him and his workmen another five years finally to close the breach. His memorial must be that stout sea wall and the Ford factory itself, which would not be there but for Perry's persistence.

DANBURY 1

In the twilight of a summer's evening we pushed the door of Danbury church and it yielded to our touch. A church which can be left unlocked is a happy discovery these days. In the failing light it seemed to gather holiness and mystery. We walked the more quietly, spoke in whispers of our pleasure at the sight of the beautifully carved bench-ends where animals stood out in the round. It was interesting to find that this was largely modern work in harmony with a couple of very old benches at the back.

Then in niches under windows either side of the church we saw life-size effigies of knights, carved in wood. The carver is unknown, the subjects, crusaders who came home to die in their own country, are unknown; what remains to modern eyes is the beauty of the work, the feeling that the sculptor infused into the formal postures of these three figures. Home again, we looked up the story of those 700-year-old monuments and found that, back in 1779, during repairs, one of the coffins below an effigy was opened and the corpse was found to be almost perfectly preserved in a liquid which Mr White, one of several interested bystanders, tasted and declared to be 'partaking of the taste of catsup, and of the pickle of Spanish olives'. It is reassuring to read that the coffin was respectfully closed and re-deposited.

DANBURY 2

A sign on the main road to Danbury from Chelmsford points a way down a drive to the Anglian Regional Management Centre. Dull it seems, yet it has history. The drive winds round to a large house where modern extensions have been hidden as discreetly as possible. Yet the house itself is not very old; it was built in 1831 to the order of John Horace Round, well-known historian, who had the old 'farmhouse' on the site, Danbury Place, demolished. It had been built in Elizabethan times for Sir Walter Mildmay, then Lord of the Manor, but its beauty and its convenience had been blurred and marred by centuries of use. It was Mrs Susan Round who gave the new place its restless, mock-Tudor picturesqueness in red brick, in consultation with the architect Thomas Hopper. She insisted on an interior staircase of stone because she was unaccountably fearful of fire, and strange to relate she was killed in a fire at a London hotel when she went back upstairs for some valuable jewellery.

The Place, sold to the Church, became a Palace for the Bishop of Rochester, whose see included Essex. So it became, and still is known as Danbury Palace and a special chapel was built on in 1860. Today it is owned by the County Council and most of its gardens are a country park where the public can wander round the lakes by which His Lordship once strolled in quiet contemplation and which are the remains of the moat of a manor house which preceded even that of the Mildmays.

DEDHAM 1

Essex is proud of its association with the great artist John Constable (1776–1837). He was not born here, but crossed the bridge over the Stour beside the lock to come to school at Dedham, saying of it later, 'I love every stile and stump, and every lane in the village ...' and we are fortunate that scenes like *Dedham Vale* painted in 1811 and *Dedham Lock* have brought the beauty of our county before the eyes of millions the world over. At 19, Constable had faced the fact that he would never make a miller like his father, Golding, and had gone to London to study art; spending his summers sketching and painting in this district around Dedham.

It is strange to us to read that, although keeping the wolf from the door with portraiture, he did not sell a landscape to other than his friends until 1814. In fact, that picture which can now be seen in fifty per cent of English homes, *The Hay Wain* was actually bought by a Frenchman in 1821 as 'A Landscape — Noon'. Thankfully the National Gallery took advantage of another opportunity and bought it for the nation.

The lock here at Dedham was part of the Stour Navigation which extended inland to Sudbury, forming the county boundary from Sturmer down to the ten-mile estuary from Manningtree to Harwich. It is the scene of that painting known later as *The Leaping Horse* of 1825 and it is very satisfying to Essex people to be told by Charles Mitchell: 'For vibrant impressionism of detail, unity of sentiment and majestic coherence in the whole he perhaps never surpassed the achievement of his large study for *The Leaping Horse*.'

In 1828 Constable's financial worries were solved when he received a £20,000 legacy from his father-in-law which enabled him 'to stand before a six-foot canvas with a mind at ease, thank God'.

CAMBS

GT. CHESTERFORD
ASHDON
STEEPLE BUMPSTEAD
SAFFRON WALDEN
AUDLEY END
ARKESDEN
NEWPORT
FINCHINGFIEL
THAXTED
GT. BARDFIEL
HENHAM
ESSE
STANSTED MOUNTFITCHET
BOC
BRAINTREE
FELSTED
BISHOP'S STORTFORD
CANFIELD
DUNMOW
RAYNE
BLACK NOTLE
HERTS
HIGH RODING
LEIGHS
HATFIELD BROAD OAK
PLESHEY
HIGH EASTER
LEADEN RODING
GOOD EASTER
LITTLE WALTHA
HARLOW
ROXWELL
MATCHING
CHELMSFORD
D
WRITTLE
EPPING
CHIPPING ONGAR
MARGARETTING
WALTHAM ABBEY
INGATESTONE
CHIGWELL
MOUNTNESSING
BRENTWOOD
BILLERIC
GREATER LONDON
ROMFORD
HORNCHURCH
BASILDON
BARKING
DAGENHAM
HORNDON ON THE HILL
GRAYS
ORSETT
R
TILBURY
K

64

SUFFOLK

HADLEIGH

EY

NGTHORPE

E
GHAM

DEDHAM

River Stour

HARWICH

HALSTEAD

ARL'S COLNE

CHAPPEL COLCHESTER

REENSTED

ALDHAM

TENDRING

WALTON

COGGESHALL

COPFORD

WIVENHOE

FRINTON

VER END

FINGRINGHOE

BRIGHTLINGSEA

BOURNE

LAYER
MARNEY

TIPTREE

ST.
OSYTH

CLACTON

WITHAM

E. MERSEA

W. MERSEA

HEYBRIDGE

River Blackwater

DON

BRADWELL

ASHELDHAM

ODHAM
FERRERS

River Crouch

BURNHAM

BATTLESBRIDGE

ASHINGDON

FOULNESS
ISLAND

SOUTHEND

CANVEY ISLAND

mes

II

DEDHAM 2

Dedham has been pronounced 'The most attractive small town in Essex,' and I guess few of the thousands of British and foreign tourists who put it on their list would disagree. It is remarkable that Constable has *not* been commercialised in signs, shops or souvenirs. The church overlooks a main street where buildings of all ages harmonise, perhaps because they still perform their useful functions as shops, pubs, houses, so that, as Pevsner says: 'There is nothing at Dedham to hurt the eye ...' Let us take one example in Shermans, the house opposite the church owned by the National Trust. In its early Georgian classical style, dated around 1730, it is so like the two houses which formed the old Grammar School that it is probable they were all built by the same man. The yellowish brick of its parapeted three-storeyed facade is varied with tall pilasters each side and windows arched or framed in warm, red brick. A flight of steps leads to a white pilastered and pedimented front door over which there is a decorative niche repeating the design. Above that again, high on the parapet, is an interesting sundial in stone.

It once belonged to that Sherman family of whom one, Edmund, a clothier, in 1599, founded an English school with a house for a writing master, which was amalgamated with the much older Grammar School.

Shermans

DEDHAM 3

A quarter of a mile south of Dedham, on the side road to Ardleigh and
the A137 is a private residence which must get a mention in a book of
this nature because it speaks history to those prepared to learn its
language. Southfields was built around 1500 for one of the clothiers,
that is, dealers in cloth, who made fortunes out of Essex wool. It is a
timber-framed construction originally plastered but with some beams
exposed, forming a quadrangle with access under a big gable supported
on exposed beams and brackets.

Mr G. H. Rendall in *Dedham in History* deals with the local legend that
Southfields was a Bay and Say Mill, or cloth factory — 'it was never a
factory, but the business residence, storehouse and offices of a leading
clothier, of the Sherman family ... It is admirably adapted to site and
purpose. The handsome corner fronting South and West, was the owner's
dwelling-house; the East front, facing towards the King's Highway for
convenience of cartage, was the storage warehouse for finished goods;
the Ground Floor housed cartsheds and equipment, while the Upper
Floor, approached by exterior flights of steps, was devoted to storage ...'
The gatehouse on the north side was adjoined by counting house and
offices. But trade declined and it became, from 1742 to 1820, more
of a home than a business to the Blomfield family.

EARLS COLNE

The largest of the villages taking half their name from the river which made their settlement possible, Earls Colne can boast of a number of timber-framed houses and a church which, though much restored in 1884, has its origin at least as far back as the 14th century, on the evidence of the windows in the south aisle. Another ancient foundation is its grammar school. The great De Vere family valued this lordship and endowed a priory of Benedictine monks early in the 12th century — it gave the village status and a school would have been a natural adjunct even before the accepted date of its foundation in 1520, when Christopher Swallow, Vicar of Messing, bequeathed lands to provide a schoolmaster 'learned in the Latin tongue ...' By 1592 it was necessary to re-let the lands because they were only bringing in £9 per annum — not enough to attract a decent schoolmaster!

The ups and downs of the school through all the years have been ably chronicled by Mr A. D. Merson in his *History* ..., including its closure in 1883 and its re-organisation and re-opening four years later by the Charity Commissioners. By 1893, through the generosity of local men of note like Reuben Hunt and J. Augustus Towell, a completely new school was built in York Road. Hunt's £6,000 contribution to build a house for the headmaster and thirty pupils to mark Victoria's Diamond Jubilee was noted in a report to the Essex County Council in 1905 — 'In no other case in the county of Essex has an individual benefactor done so much in recent years to resuscitate an old foundation and to bring its buildings and equipment to a high level of efficiency ...'

This constant rebuilding and modernising went on up to the last war and continued after it, ready for the record number of 258 scholars in 1958. In 1972 history was made when a *girl* was admitted. And so the ancient foundation, changing with the times, has survived into a totally new age of education — and with the blessing of the Secretary of State it is still holding its own.

Earls Colne School around 1900

EPPING 1

In the whole of Epping Forest there is only one personal memorial stone
other than that to Sir Winston Churchill at Woodford. It was set up before
the rule of exclusion was introduced. Situated in the middle of Walthamstow Forest, yet within sound of the North Circular Road, this stone
marks the spot where a gipsy, Rodney Smith, was born in a caravan in
1860. Let the Methodist Recorder of 10th August 1978 take up the story:
'A memorial service to Gypsy Smith thirty one years after his death was
held in the heart of Epping Forest on Friday at his birthplace ... It was
his own wish that his ashes be laid in the venue of his humble beginnings ...
This service of remembrance and thanksgiving [was] for his seventy years
of preaching in five continents ...'

Gipsy Smith's conversion and subsequent life of evangelism began
in 1876 when, as a 16-year-old lad he attended a Primitive Methodist
meeting. Shortly afterwards he followed William Booth in becoming one
of the first officers of the Salvation Army, which he left in 1882 to carry
on a personal crusade of evangelism, drawing crowds around the world
with the power of his preaching. He died in 1947 on a trans-Atlantic
liner.

EPPING 2

Though it stands on the edge of the modern county and much nearer
Chingford than Epping, Queen Elizabeth's Hunting Lodge is entered here
not for its geographical location but for its place in the history of Epping
Forest. That place is modern as well as ancient.

The timbered three-storeyed building was once completely open at
the top with a cambered floor which still exists to allow the rain to drain
away. The second storey was also left open, but for the framing, to form
a comfortable 'stand' from which the forest and its animals could be
observed. It is thought to have been built early in the 16th century and it
is not difficult to dress it in the mind with the richly costumed company
of Elizabethan courtiers which would arrive on horseback from London
for a gay day in the woods. The smaller arm of the L-shaped lodge forms
a staircase round an open well.

Its modern function is as 'a museum dedicated to preserving the story
and the life of Epping Forest'. All kinds of objects from flint implements
to man-traps illustrate that story, and the results of archaeological
excavations at the ancient British camps of Loughton and Ambresbury
Banks are separately displayed. In the Oak Room upstairs and the room
above, the natural history of the Forest is represented.

FAULKBOURNE

When an architectural expert like Nikolaus Pevsner says, 'Several nice
cottages in the village street', you can guess that ordinary mortals like me
find it a charming place. That is how I feel about Faulkbourne, not so
much for the cottages as for the swampy, overgrown pond which borders
the road between Home Farm and the church. Do not let its present
appearance fool you; it is a very ancient, holy spot, a real wishing well;
for ancient man addressed his entreaties to the God of Water as the giver
of life. Its power persisted in the popular mind into medieval times when
this spring became quite famous as a healing well and pilgrims between
Bury St Edmunds and Canterbury strayed from their route to visit it.
It was dedicated, like the church, to the missionary Bishop St German.

We find this place recorded in the Domesday Book as Falcheburna —
'the folk's stream' and Church and Hall still stand with it as three
features of the Saxon settlement. The present St German's can still show
its Norman origin in nave and chancel, and Faulkbourne Hall is just about
the finest 15th-century mansion in the county — rambling, red-brick,
gabled, towered and battlemented.

FELSTED

The church of the Holy Cross is hemmed in by houses, but it is no modern development which brought that about. The house which blocks its approach, apart from a coaching-inn kind of entrance, was built five hundred years ago! In its upper storey, running over the churchyard gate, there began the school founded by Richard, Lord Rich, who made a fortune serving Henry VIII in the dissolution of the monasteries. Though still called the Old Schoolhouse, it was superseded in 1866 as was the nearby New Schoolhouse designed by John Johnson in 1800 and now called Ingrams. It numbered among its scholars three sons of Oliver Cromwell. By Victorian times Felsted was established as a reputable public school and it is from the re-building in 1866, designed by Frederick Chancellor, later Mayor of Chelmsford, that the complex of modern buildings has grown. Church and School are but examples of the interesting architecture which lines the two main streets, including the oft-quoted house built by George Boot in 1596 as explained by an inscription on the bressumer or main horizontal beam. Rich was brought from his great house at Little Leighs to be buried in the church in 1568, under a monument, rich indeed, set up to him and to his son who died in 1581, by his grandson as late as 1620, in the style and probably by the hand of the famous Epiphanius Evesham.

FINCHINGFIELD

Finchingfield earns a place in this book as the long-suffering, much-photographed, 'prettiest village in Essex'. When one stands at the bottom of the hill over the bridge and looks across the pond and its water fowl to the white-washed houses climbing the street to the Guildhall where the church pokes its strong tower and tiny cupola up into the sky it is easy to see how it gained the accolade.

It is under the long, white, timber-framed Guildhall where a museum is currently growing and village societies meet, that there is an archway to the churchyard. So one comes suddenly upon the church to gaze with head thrown back at the bulk of a tower built in early Norman times — some four hundred years before anyone thought of the Guildhall.

On a tablet in the church will be found an inscription recording the death of William Kemp, 1555–1628, whose only claim to fame was his vow, after falsely accusing his wife of inconstancy, never to speak another word for seven years. Though his wife died in 1623 he kept his vow to the bitter end. In fact, Sir William Addison tells us: 'At the end of the period he was in such a state of agitation that he became ill, and when he tried to call for help found himself powerless to utter a sound. The shock killed him.' Seven fish ponds, of which two now form the lake at his old home of Spains Hall, were said to have been excavated one by one to mark each year of silence, but I have a feeling there is more fiction than fact in the legend.

FINGRINGHOE

When the Romans conquered the British at Colchester and established a colony, they needed a port to bring in supplies and it seems they chose Fingringhoe as the nearest navigable place on the Colne from the open sea. So they built a fort there to protect it and its site is marked on present day maps right beside another legend, 'Nature Reserve', which brings the history of the place right up to date. Its centre is away to the west where traces have been found of prehistoric settlement, though its name comes from later, Saxon settlement as 'the place of the dwellers on the finger of land' — between Geedon Creek and Roman River.

St Andrew's brings the story on to Norman times in its nave, and the 14th century in its chancel. The shell of the old Hall shows an Early Georgian remodelling of a 17th-century brick facade with interesting gables.

Looking at the perfect setting of the church by the pond, amid the trees with that hoary giant, the Fingringhoe Oak, prominent and a lovely further view, it is hard to imagine that St Andrew's was very badly damaged in the great Essex earthquake of 1884. The Nature Reserve was set up in 1961 by the Essex Naturalists' Trust, the first of 34 sites acquired by this active, public-spirited body whose information centre is here at Fingringhoe Wick.

Wilson, Bowers, Seaman, Evans, Scott and Oates
at the South Pole, 18 January 1912

GESTINGTHORPE

'A long, straggling village on high ground', says the 1887 *Handbook* which then dismisses Gestingthorpe in seven lines. But there is a later history to the place, in that someone famous lived in its Hall, as can be seen from a brass plate on the north wall of the nave of St Mary's. It was placed there by officers of the Inniskilling Dragoons as a memorial to Captain Oates who died during Scott's Antarctic expedition in1912.

The story goes back to 1891, the year that 11-year-old Lawrence Oates and his family came to live at Gestingthorpe Hall. He eventually joined the army and the next clue to his career is found high up in the Tudor brick belfry where the fifth and sixth bells are inscribed as having been recast in 1901 at Mrs Oates' expense in gratitude to God for her son's safe return from the South African war.

Ten years later he was so pleased to be selected by Scott for his ill-fated expedition to the South Pole. They got there but found Amunsden had beaten them to it by a month. They trudged back in appalling weather, with Oates a very sick man. Scott's diary recorded: 'he was a brave soul. He slept through the night, hoping not to wake, but he awoke in the morning. It was blowing a blizzard. Oates said: "I am just going outside, and I may be some time." We knew he was walking to his death; but though we tried to dissuade him, we knew it was the act of a brave man and an English gentleman.' Oates knew that he was a hindrance to the party's progress — but fate decreed that all should die. The brass tablet shows that Lawrence Edward Grace Oates died on 17th March 1912 — his 32nd birthday.

75

GREAT BARDFIELD

Great Bardfield is a village which can look back on a much more important past, when its ancient green was transformed by expansion into a
triangle of streets with the base along the B1057 from Dunmow as it
comes up to the bridge over the Pant. In those days it had a charter to
hold a market and a fair, and some of the old houses, so handy now for
antique shops, reflect in size and architecture that early importance.

It was just a sleepy village before the war, when it became the site of
a remarkable experiment in the training and rehabilitation of 'wayward
adolescents'. Hawkspur Camp started in May 1936, a tented community
in a field where it was hoped that young people who had kicked over the
traces might learn self-discipline rather than the Discipline of Borstal.
It was not recognized officially and within four years it had been closed
because of the war, but it showed the way to the modern method of
Planned Environmental Therapy and takes its place in the history of social
work.

After the war, Great Bardfield gained considerable status from the
colony of artists who pursued their individual styles in friendly juxtapo-
sition, including John Aldridge, Michael Rothenstein, Edward Bawden and
other well-known artists.

Today one of the smallest houses in Great Bardfield is its biggest
attraction. In the High Street stands a cottage which was built in Elizabethan times as an alms-house. It served its purpose up to 1958 when it
was condemned by modern living standards. Local people urged preservation and so, in 1961, after careful restoration and an appeal for suitable
objects, it became Bardfield Cottage Museum, open at weekends, with
special emphasis on corn dollies.

GREAT CANFIELD

A cul-de-sac village must be a great place to live in, no through traffic,
road junctions, ugly signs, and no noise; but the trouble with Great
Canfield is that at its centre, by the church, there is not much room
for houses either. There was not much need for them when this tiny
hamlet was first formed in the shadow of a wooden castle keep on the
palisaded mound rising 45ft above a moat plentifully filled by the river
Roding. It was reared up by the powerful De Vere family, soon after
the Norman conquest, to protect their newly-acquired manor.

The Church was built on its northwest edge at the same time and, but
for the addition of a belfry under a shingled spire and a south porch of
stone, remains in its Norman state. That includes, within, a striking
chancel arch, so wide and smoothly round; on one side the top of the
column incorporates a Saxon grave slab. The point of interest which
continues to attract pilgrims is the 13th-century wall painting in an arched
recess over the altar of the Virgin Mary and her child Jesus. The
tenderness and piety expressed by an unknown artist are conveyed to us
across eight hundred years. There are other features which offer peaceful pleasure, from the Wiseman monuments to the setting of the church
itself, in company with pretty houses and the Hall beyond.

GREAT CHESTERFORD

There is nothing in Great Chesterford today to give a clue to its former lofty status. Perhaps the straightness of the A130 and the A11 after the Stumps Cross roundabout are enough to suggest Roman activity — and this is the answer. This village was once a Roman town replacing a British settlement on a bend in the Cam (or Granta) river. In the 4th century its 36acre extent was entirely walled round and pierced with three gateways, and the only other town I know to be thus defended is Colchester. But we should not imagine cohorts of stiff-necked soldiers stamping about the fort which had been established here in the 1st century. After three hundred years of occupation the native British had adopted Roman ways, costume, language. Of their town only two substantial buildings have been excavated — and one of them has been identified as a tax office! The huddle of houses were of wood and wattle and daub — not a bit like the impressive Colchester town centre.

In the 18th century parts of the walls were standing, but they were soon used up in the making up of the roads round about to solve the growing traffic problem. Yet so many coins of that Roman period still lay about the Borough Field that the landlord of the local inn was selling them as souvenirs at twopence a time. Today's souvenir-hunters would be disappointed. The whole site was excavated in 1948 — for gravel!

GREAT DUNMOW

A small town, far away from London influence, it still has the homo-geneity, the small-is-beautiful air which makes people glad to be its burgesses. There are many points of interest for the visitor, from the bacon factory at one end, reminder of the Flitch ceremony recently revived here, to the Church at the other. Between the two can be seen a pleasant main street, with a free car park off it, many interesting shops, several old houses and the Old Town Hall of 1578 at the junction which once formed the market place.

Just beyond that is the Doctor's Pond which laps at the very edge of the street. It got its name from a much-loved local physician, Dr Rayner, who died in 1804 aged 54. He used to play bowls with the local gentry in the garden of the house above the pond, then called The Bowling Green, and the proper maintenance of the pond became his concern, to the extent that he even stocked it with fish. It was on this village pond, far away from any ocean, that the first models of a self-righting lifeboat were tried out in 1785. The inventor was Lionel Lukin, a coach builder of Long Acre, who was born here, the youngest son of William Lukin, of Blatches, Little Dunmow, in 1742. His tombstone at Hythe, Kent, dated 1834, describes him as 'the inventor of the lifeboat principle'.

GREAT WALTHAM 1

The 'homestead in the forest' named by the Saxons is known to us as Waltham, Great and Little. Up to recent times the dividing line was down the middle of Little Waltham's main street, so it would only be fair to claim for Great Waltham the extensive Iron Age village which flourished on the vale sloping down to the river Chelmer. Then our village saw Romans, Saxons and Normans leave their mark. It is a very simple item which brings those Romano-British folk of fifteen hundred years and more ago oh! so close — a leather sandal, with a broken strap, found in the sediment of a Roman well. How annoyed *we* are when a shoelace breaks!

Life here persisted, became complicated, people moved about, traffic increased and roads, by the 18th century became broken-down quagmires. Something had to be done! So tollgates were set up on stretches of main roads so that their repair might be financed by their users. There was one at Ash Tree Corner on the A130, and as gatekeepers had to live on the job a tiny, timber and tile tollhouse was put up by the gate. By the middle of the 19th century railways made tollgates redundant and the little house, no longer needed there, was bought by some enterprising house-hunter and literally loaded on to a cart and transported to its present position beside the lane westwards to Broads Green.

GREAT WALTHAM 2

A charming white-painted lodge on the A130 at the approach to the village
guards the gate to Langleys. It is said that it was built as a miniature re-
production of the facade of the big house, and it does bear a similar
colourful coat of arms on its pediment. Morant, writing in 1768, traces
a mansion on this site back to King John's reign and shows that the
Langleys owned it some time during the reign of Edward II (died 1377),
but the great family name here is Everard; they 'seated themselves here,
and many years made a considerable figure'. That was in 1515 and their
ownership over a century is evidenced in the grand monument of 1611
in the church. A century later an impecunious scion sold it to Samuel
Tufnell, 29-year-old London business man and Member of Parliament,
who set about rebuilding the place to his own tasteful standards, though
he preserved two rooms where the decoration remains to this day as it
was in about 1620. They are the Library and the former Dining Room,
where the richness of the plasterwork is nationally notable.

A later Tufnell redesigned rooms at the end of the 18th century like
the White Drawing Room where furniture and decoration were all of a
piece and can still be seen. The house is lived in privately but the gardens
are often open to the public in aid of charity, and the park which fronts
the house has a right-of-way through it which makes a pleasant stroll to
the other side of the village, with a walk back past all the old houses,
the Church of St Mary and St Laurence and the Six Bells to complete
a circular tour.

GREENSTED-JUXTA-ONGAR

There are Roman remains in the field beside St Andrew's church, but just for once they go un-noticed and unexcavated because the church itself, a thousand years younger, outshines the scatter of Roman brick and tile. St Andrew's is the only surviving wooden-built Saxon church in our country. It had been accepted for years that it was put up to shelter the corpse of St Edmund as it was being carried from London to Bury St Edmunds in 1013, but scientific tests push the date back to the middle of the 9th century which brings before our eyes the vision of devoted Christian Saxons hacking a clearing in the forest and building their church from the very trees they had chopped down. The walls were formed with limbs of oak split in halves and set up in cills made of trunks laid horizontally on the ground.

Of course, the little church has undergone much restoration and repair but those great oak timbers survive in the nave, standing now on a brick plinth of 1848. The charming dormer windows which give the church a cottage air were inserted in the 16th century when the chancel was built in brick. At the other end, a white-painted timber tower is crowned with a small shingled spire. Its internal construction is all of wooden beams and has been dated as far apart as the 14th and 17th centuries.

HADLEIGH

Talking of the artist John Constable, A. C. Edwards, in his, *History of Essex* says: 'Among his other Essex works, his *Wivenhoe Park* and *Hadleigh Castle* are outstanding.' Would Constable find that Castle ruin as outstanding today? There has been so much development since he died in 1837 that he might well lose his way. But once at the Castle he would find the larger, wider view south across the tip of Canvey Island and the Thames to the Kentish heights very much the same. And there is still a considerable green about the Castle.

Hubert de Burgh, already mentioned under Brentwood, was, in 1231, granted a licence by the King to build 'a certain castle at Hadlee' but within the year he had fallen from grace and the castle then under construction passed to Henry III who had it completed and installed governors whose most onerous duty was to have the place ready for royal hunting parties. When the French became aggressive in the reign of Edward III (1327–77) it was largely rebuilt to protect the passage up the Thames. This was its period of greatest glory. Danger passed, money became shorter and the mighty bastion slowly crumbled. By 1551 the powerful Lord Rich was able to buy this desirable property from Edward VI for £700 but he had his eye on its value simply as building material which was carted round the county to build churches and houses.

So it was a ruin when Constable came to it, though more has been lost since then in a landslip. Now it is preserved as an ancient monument. It had no great keep; the remains we see are chiefly the big towers to northeast and southeast, the latter being the object of Constable's brush.

HALSTEAD

Park in the High Street, or in the free car park off it, and you will find that Halstead has a good deal to offer. For one thing it is a pleasant shopping place, for another, no-one is going to make you poke about in Roman ruins — there are none! And there are no reminders either of the Saxons whose 'healthy place' gave the town its name. They would have built the first church, but the present one dates from the 14th century, with an attractive square, battlemented, pinnacled tower built in 1848, after a long period of neglect. One of the bells within is of the original 16th-century peal and connects with the bellringer's jar kept in the belfry which is dated 1658 and inscribed: 'In summer heat and winter cold, to drink of this we dare be bold. If you be wise, fill me not twice, at one sitting.' Very good advice, since it can hold four and a half gallons!

It was here in 1782 that George Courtauld set up a weaving mill across the Colne, along The Causeway. That big, white, clapboard mill is still operating, though the river no longer has a hand in it.

HARLOW 1

A century-old guide sums up Old Harlow: 'An ancient town on the Stort, formerly of greater importance than now, once having a market and being a seat of the woollen manufacture. It consists of one long street, with many ancient houses.' The place has not changed much, but that street has been pedestrianised — an ugly word for a happy circumstance. Now shopping can be a pleasure and one can pause to raise one's eyes to the interesting architecture above all the brash business show. Although some new building was necessary, a surprising amount of Georgian work is seen to be surviving; a striking contrast to the New Harlow west and south.

It would have been pleasing to have the church as the centrepiece of all the ancient building, but since the original building was almost totally destroyed by fire in April 1708, rebuilt the following year, and then rebuilt again in 1880, as we see it, it hardly qualifies for that honour. But in the north transept of St Mary's a large number of interesting brasses from that medieval church have been brought together, ranging in date over two centuries from about 1430.

The oldest Harlow of which we have evidence is the Roman town which seems to have lasted some three hundred years from about 50 AD and is indicated by the Romano-Celtic temple 250yds west of the railway station, excavated in 1927.

HARLOW 2

It was on 25th March 1947 that an order under the New Towns Act set aside 6320 acres of land in the parishes of Harlow, Great and Little Parndon, Latton and Netteswell to form the site for the new town of Harlow. After thirty years it is still called Harlow New Town, but it now has a history behind it, and a geography, for a population numbered in hundreds in those individual villages has swelled to the 80,000 mark, requiring accommodation, services and facilities. The Harlow Development Corporation was set up to see the grand design brought to completion. Its new coat of arms reflects the owning of these lands in former times by the monasteries — including the Bury St Edmund crowns, the Waltham cross and the Beeleigh fleur de lis crowned by a crest combining the griffin of Latton Priory holding one Essex seaxe, and all finished off with the motto 'Members one of another'. This sentiment is fully realised in the planning of The High, the heart of the new body, where all can share the shopping and entertainment, embracing unusual items like the water gardens by the Town Hall and the view from its tower of this town in the countryside which the renowned town planner Frederick Gibberd master-minded. It has been further beautified by works of art, mostly sculptures by contemporary artists like Henry Moore, Barbara Hepworth and Lynn Chadwick which have been set up in appropriate places by the Harlow Trust. This is one place on which readers can get all the extra information they need, from postcard to Master Plan, by writing to the Information Officer.

HARWICH 1

How are the mighty fallen! The Great Eastern Hotel, overlooking the very quay to which the boats brought an endless stream of rich guests, was built in 1864 — a rapid erection in all the breathless haste of the railway age, for the railhead itself only reached the town in 1862 and that hotel, designed by Thomas Allom, ran to five storeys of white brick, in a style which borrowed from the Italian but ranged freely through the architectural spectrum with a classical pediment, some baroque flourishes, and an air of confidence hardly in keeping with its short-lived glory. By 1883 the continental ferry boats had left Harwich for Parkeston and the hotel assumed an air of suffering neglect. It remained an expensive memorial to those breezy days of railway riches right down to 1936 when it was bought by the Council, whose plans for its conversion were thwarted by the war.

By 1951 the Borough of Harwich had been able to restore and convert the hotel into a commodious and convenient Town Hall where, in 1958, Her Majesty the Queen and Prince Philip were entertained before they boarded the Royal Yacht for a state visit to Holland. The 1974 Re-organisation made Harwich merely part of the Tendring District Council, but the good old Great Eastern continues as the offices of the Chief Technical Officer for the District.

HARWICH 2

How many Kings and Queens of England have thankfully set foot on
Harwich soil after a rough North Sea voyage! Their Hanoverian connec-
tions in the 18th century and after brought much traffic across the water,
and it was safeguarded by all the safety devices then available, including
lighthouses to beam a nightly guide. The High and Low lighthouses had
become decrepit, so they were rebuilt in 1818 to designs by John Rennie,
and though rendered quite redundant by modern methods of navigation,
they have been allowed to survive as reminders of the courage and determination of an earlier generation of fishermen and packetmasters.

In early times these lighthouses were leased out for individuals to make
what profit they could from the shipping using their light, so at Harwich
the Rebow family reaped a rich reward. In 1812 the Borough petitioned
the Lords of the Treasury that they might be assigned the lease and use
the money to improve the town, but the Rebows were granted it once
again on condition that they rebuilt the lighthouses and ceded three-
fifths of the profits to the crown. Though it cost £8,000 to rebuild the
lighthouses it should be placed against the £159,730 paid in compensation
by Trinity house when taking over the lighthouse service in 1836.

HARWICH 3

With the re-organisation of boundaries in 1974 Parkeston, so long outside the Borough of Harwich, became part of the same District, so all that old feeling about the railway taking its ferry business from the town can be forgotten. It was in 1883 that the new Parkeston Quay terminal was opened. The reason has been clearly set out in Leonard Weaver's *The Harwich Story* (1975).

The Great Eastern Railway, which came this way in 1862, was welcomed with joy by Harwich people looking for jobs and business opportunities, but it was the very expansion of trade with Europe which found the limited facilities of the old port wanting. There was no space on that Harwich headland to develop the waterfront sufficiently. The Royal Navy had come to the same decision about their Navy Yard here in 1713. There has also been a claim that the railway company did not agree with the increase in coal dues demanded by the Borough. The G.E.R. moved its main station two miles up the Stour to Ray Island where the Quay was named Parkeston after the chairman of the company, Charles H. Parkes. So, as Leonard Weaver says: 'No longer did unfortunate passengers from Antwerp disembark at Harwich at 2am and struggle with their baggage through wind and rain up George Street to catch the boat train which left for Liverpool Street at 3am.'

HATFIELD BROAD OAK

Hatfield Broad Oak is a village of great charm where houses of all periods gather round the junction by the village pump which has been described as having 'all the elegance of a Georgian coffee pot'. It is likely that houses huddled here following the establishment of a Benedictine Priory by Alberic de Vere, first Earl of Oxford, in 1135 on the demesne lands of the Conqueror himself, hence its early name of King's Hatfield, though the remarkably large oak tree was being quoted at the beginning of the 12th century.

It was in 1378 that the villagers actually attacked the monks in a row over the upkeep of their part of the church. King Richard II judged the issue and said that the monks' choir and the altar must be separated from the villagers' part of the church by a strong wall, and that wall stands as the east end of the present parish church of St Mary the Virgin which was rebuilt in the 15th century in perpendicular style. Sometime after the Dissolution the monastery passed into the hands of the Barrington family as a private residence and the monastery church was demolished. The 13th-century effigy of Robert de Vere was preserved in the parish church where it can still be seen, though a good deal the worse for wear. Still in good condition is the library founded by vicar George Stirling in 1708 in a room specially built for it at the expense of Sir Charles Barrington. Lovely brown leather-covered books on philosophy, theology, history and biography, include both a 'breeches' and a 'vinegar' Bible.

HENHAM

Henham-on-the-Hill has a cosy ring about it, and even today, with the inevitable modern fringe of houses it keeps that warmth with a wide-spreading, pretty village green and large old houses with vestiges of their moated origins in pools and ponds which reflect the tranquil scene. But it is not pastoral beauty or architectural interest which claim our atten-tion, it is the strange case of the Henham dragon.

Miller Christy, celebrated in our county as naturalist and historian, came across a pamphlet in the British Museum touching on 'The Flying Serpent, or, Strange News out of Essex, being a true relation of a monstrous serpent which hath divers times been seen at a Parish called Henham-on-the-Mount ...' That was in 1669, so it was no unsupported fairy tale. It included a likeness of the serpent down to its arrow-head tail as seen by the seven sober citizens, including the Churchwarden and Constable who appended their names as witnesses. It was in May that the serpent first threatened a rider along by the Birch Wood. 'Not long after two men of the same Parish walking that way, espy'd this Serpent as he lay on a Hillock ... being as near as they could guess 8 or 9 foot long ... his eyes were very large and piercing ... and on his back he had two wings indifferent large ... altogether too weak to carry such an unwieldy body ...' From then on it appeared to any number of people, doing no harm, though it seems they were always bent on its destruction. But it was too quick in retreating to the deep woods to be killed and survived even as the pamphlet went to print because 'The report of this Serpent is so terrible to the inhabitants thereabout that no women, children, nay nor a great many men durst not go near the place where he lurks, yet we hear not of any mischief that he has done, though it be a wonder to most people on what he subsists ...'

HEYBRIDGE

When Tid settled his Saxon kin here in the woody marshes to give the place a name — Tidwoldington, he could never have imagined that a great, high bridge would be built across the river, or that the river itself would form part of a 14mile-long canal. The place became better known as High Bridge or Heybridge in Norman times from the five-arched stone bridge which spanned the Blackwater. At the same time the church of St Andrew was built in its basic form. The tower, added later, was undermined by the great flood around 1450 and collapsed on to the nave, reducing it to a ruin, but rebuilding was completed by the end of the century and is the church as we see it.

Heybridge's maritime character comes out strongly at the Basin, the last lock on the canal using the water of the Chelmer and the Blackwater. Here the Jolly Sailor lies well below the stout sea wall where steps give on to the towpath beside a great pool dammed by the massive gates which outwit the ebbing tide. The cutting of the Chelmer and Blackwater Navigation from 1793 was fraught with difficulties but Richard Coates, Resident Engineer, overcame them and from its opening on 3rd June 1797 it made a good profit from barge traffic until hit by competition from the railway around 1845, and as railways also out-priced coastal shipping, the traffic on the canal fell even more from 1866 to its total stoppage in 1972. But the company then introduced, from 1975, an entirely new idea of public participation in this watery amenity. Small boats can be moored and driven all along the canal from Chelmsford to Heybridge Basin, and a large cruising vessel is provided to take parties on tours of the old canal with refreshments available on board.

HORNCHURCH

Hornchurch is no longer in the re-defined county of Essex, but it was when great things were happening there in the dark days of the Second World War. Then it was an aerodrome from which fighters flew to challenge the menace of hundreds of German bombers. During the Battle of Britain, spanning a month from 12th August 1940, the Hornchurch fighter squadrons destroyed 164 enemy aircraft, not without loss of course. During the war the aerodrome was attacked twentythree times. On one occasion Spitfires taking off were hit by the blast from bombs and three pilots were literally blown out of their planes, yet survived to go into action again the next day. The whole story of this small but vital 'drome has been told by Sqdn Ldr H. T. Sutton in *Raiders approach* (1956).

No-one seeing the development of the area today would imagine that it was from this patch of grass that 2nd Lieut Sowrey took off in his BE2c one September night in 1916 to seek out and destroy the Zeppelin which fell at Great Burstead. The station was disbanded in 1919 and within eighteen months the runways were under the plough. Lord Trenchard, however, maintained that London's defence needed this air-field and he got it back into use in 1928. How right he was proved to be!

The Open Days and air displays of Empire Air days from 1935 were all too quickly given up for the real thing. It was on 15th September 1940, the very day appointed by Hitler for the invasion of Britain, that Horn-church Spitfires downed fifteen enemy aircraft. Such courage won the war and thankfully the station could again be stood down, first to a training function until 1962 and then completely and for good. Then the Royal Air Force said goodbye to Hornchurch, presenting their station badge into the honourable custody of Havering Council, and the land has now been developed so that never again will London be able to look to this former Essex village for its defence.

93

HORNDON-ON-THE-HILL

The planners report that 'The old village of Horndon-on-the-Hill consists basically of one linear street, a number of small passages or alleyways and an open area around the church'. This is accurate, but hardly inviting, yet if it were not for the Village Policy Plans produced by the County Planning Department, development of new building and maintenance of the old would not be the success it is and Horndon has benefited from the exercise. The County Council makes grants to help owners of historic buildings keep their properties in good order and the Old Market Hall was so aided. It is a 16th-century building with three little casement windows under an old tiled roof with gable ends. Within are the oak posts and curved brackets which supported the upper floor when it was originally open underneath as a 'pillared market house' — an auction room for the wool trade where sales held each year brought buyers even from overseas. It is believed that the Bell and the Swan were built in those days of Horndon's prosperity.

The Essex wool trade fell away so the owner, William Kingsman, used the building to house poor widows, and so it continued through the years, acting also as a public meeting place until 1955 when it was ruled unfit for further habitation. In 1969 the local authority, concerned about its condition, granted £10,000 for its restoration and it continues as a social and cultural centre. In this village there are more than a dozen buildings, including the church of course, which are listed as of historical and architectural interest.

INGATESTONE

The Saxon for 'The people who live by the great stone' gave the modern Ing-at-stone. The stone itself may still exist in the little pieces seen either side of the lane to Fryerning. Further along the main street, a demolition of old cottages allowed a beautiful view across a green lawn of the warm, red, Tudor brick tower of St Edmund and St Mary's which has a south chapel of the same material built for the repose of generations of the local ruling family of the Petres.

Sir William Petre started the dynasty here by buying the land confiscated from Barking Abbey at the Dissolution, in 1539, pulling down the mean house on it and in the next ten years building Ingatestone Hall, 'very fair, large and stately, made of brick and embattled', in which, in 1561, Queen Elizabeth was royally entertained. The grand plan embraced an inner courtyard with the main buildings round it and two other courtyards nearer the road, one of them formed by the gatehouse and outbuildings. The great hall was demolished early in the last century, but the rest of the place is still largely as it was built and makes a marvellous picture, though cameras are not allowed down the drive because the Hall is still lived in by that same Petre family. The public are allowed to use it to get to the north wing which is leased to the Essex County Council. Here, on two floors, in and out of the old rooms, flows an exhibition, changed annually, of all kinds of material from the Essex Record Office on some aspect of Essex life and landscape. It is on show all through the summer months, as is the Long Gallery upstairs where many family portraits and some fine furniture are to be viewed.

LAYER MARNEY

The Marneys were a rich and influential family. When they took over land at Layer in the reign of Henry II they gave their name to the place and Layer Marney it is known as today. The family tombs dating from 1414, in the church they had rebuilt about 1500, are very impressive, with life-size alabaster or terra cotta effigies. Their house was to have been even more impressive. This was in the days when Henry Marney, faithful servant of Henry VIII, was rewarded with a peerage in 1523. Naturally the Lord Marney wanted to make a splash, so he put in hand a mansion beside the church which was to have, for a start, an eight-storeyed gate-house with four towers, the highest in the county. It was a status symbol with nothing behind it, for though that gatehouse was built and still stands, Lord Marney died the same year and with the death of his son in 1525 the line became extinct. Since it is open to the public from April to October on certain afternoons the 'combination of typically English design and brickwork with Italian terra cotta window frames' can be enjoyed at close quarters. It dwarfs the present Hall and the Church in Tudor brick, red with blue diaper pattern, which has many interesting features, not the least those splendid family monuments.

LITTLE DUNMOW

A village so small that it lives in the shadow of its Great neighbour has one claim to fame which justifies its inclusion. Back in 1104 the wife or sister of Ralph Baynard, the new Norman Lord of the Manor, founded a prior here and charged it with the provision, every year, of a flitch of bacon to faithful married couples. The earliest award on record is in 1444 when, after close questioning of his connubial bliss throughout the year, Richard Wright of Bradbourne in Norfolk was declared winner of the Flitch of Bacon.

The intention of the award is summed up by this early verse:

'You shall swear by custom of confession,
That you ne'er made nuptial transgression;
Nor since you were married man and wife,
By household brawls, or contentious strife,
Or otherwise, at bed or board,
Offended each other in deed or in word;
Or since the parish clerk said, Amen,
Wished yourselves unmarried again;
Or in a twelvemonth and a day,
Repented, even in thought, any way;
But continued true, in thought and desire,
As when you joined hands in holy quire.
If to these condition, without all fear,
Of your own accord you will freely swear,
A whole flitch of bacon you shall receive,
And bear it hence with love and good leave ...'

In the church, which was formed from the south aisle of the original priory chapel, there is kept a chair mounted on long shafts, which is said to be the very one used to carry high and successful contestants in triumphant procession round churchyard and village.

LITTLE LEIGHS

It is apposite that Layer Marney Towers and Leez Priory should be adjacent in this book since they were both built by Tudor statesmen and both have only the gatehouse standing to speak of past glories. About two miles due northwest of the Norman church, Leez Priory was founded in 1229 by Sir Ralph Gernon for Augustine canons. 'It stood ... in the extreme part of the parish adjoining Felsted and had large and stately buildings and an extensive park and gardens; at the Dissolution in 1536, it was valued at £141.14s.8d.' But it was not the Priory that was remarkable; it was what happened to it when it was granted by Henry VIII to his loyal servant Sir Richard Rich, Solicitor-General, who was raised to the peerage in 1547. He chose the title of Baron Rich of Leez and, tearing down the Priory, he built a vast mansion here in which his family, created Earls of Warwick, lived grandly for a century. It passed through the hands of the Dukes of Manchester and Buckinghamshire and finally, in the 18th century, it was bought by the governors of Guy's Hospital, when it was showing its age. They demolished all of it in 1753 except for the inner and outer gatehouses and parts of the outer courtyard. The outer gatehouse is all embattled but the inner is more ornately decorated, one storey higher and crowned with the original, very decorative Tudor chimney stacks.

The only chance the visitor gets of seeing these remains is when the beautiful gardens of Leez Priory are opened to the public in aid of charity.

MALDON 1

Maldon, we are told by Essex County Council, is: 'Beautifully sited at the head of the Blackwater estuary, and site of famous battle between Saxons and Danes. Many period buildings in the hilly streets including several old inns, 13th-century church (All Saints) with triangular tower that is rare in England and the 6,000 volume Plume library founded by Dr Plume in about 1700.'

The worthy doctor lived from 1630 to 1704 and was Archdeacon of Rochester for the last twentyfive years of his life. He obviously remembered his birthplace, Maldon, with affection, for he provided a workhouse and a school for it. The latter was sited on the ground floor of a two-storeyed building Plume had built against the 15th-century tower of old St Peter's church, the nave having been ruins since 1665. His will directs: 'I have erected over the school at Maldon a Library Room to which I give all my books and pictures.' Over the years the library suffered much neglect and the school moved out to better premises; but now the books are beautifully bound in leather and carefully shelved and an authoritative catalogue has been published. The Library can be visited by the public up the narrow, winding, stone staircase in the tower. When one reaches the top it is like stepping back two centuries. The range of books, with an emphasis on theology, would take days to appreciate. The oldest book dates from 1475 and the most valuable may be Milton's *Paradise Lost* and *Paradise Regained*, in their first editions — now kept in a bank vault! Books bought after the original bequest can actually be borrowed.

Nowadays the ground floor is occupied, very appropriately by the town's branch of the Essex County Library, a nice ancient and modern relationship on which I hope Dr Plume, wherever he is, smiles.

Plume Library

MALDON 2

There is a fascinating riverside, almost seaside, aspect of Maldon's character which is modern and lively yet links with the past, for St Mary's church down by the river saw marriages of fisher lads and lasses all the way from Scarborough and beyond who followed the fishing down the coast and got 'caught' themselves. Records show there was a church here before the Conquest, but the oldest parts now date from about 1130. The Norman chancel fell down around 1320 because it was built too near the edge of the steep hill down to the river. When the top of the tower collapsed in 1605 the sailors lost a good landmark, but it was rebuilt by 1635 and the beacon light was once again visible.

Behind the church, before the quay, the Jolly Sailor makes a cheerful base for walks in both directions along the riverbank. To the right a tangle of rigging, masts and spars and billowing brown sail advertises those barges for which Maldon is well known — a lingering legacy of the crowd of sailing barges blown like great butterflies around the coast from Maldon to the Thames with loads of farm produce for the London market. The promenade leads on to the recreation ground and the swimming pool where holiday-makers are as unconcerned with the flow of history as the boats which bob on the river — one of Maldon's great attractions.

MALDON 3

The old Town Hall in Maldon forces itself upon the visitor; helpfully
with a big clock projected on a bracket high above the street, and hinder-
ingly with a porch on four fat round columns striding across the pavement,
giving it such an air of authority. The porch was built about 1830, but the
Town Hall, or Moot Hall as it was known for hundreds of years, started
out as a simple tower of brick; the D'Arcy Tower, the Victorians called
it, after Robert D'Arcy who had it built in 1440. Sir Robert, as he became,
was MP for Maldon and High Sheriff of Essex and Hertfordshire in 1420.
We are told that the tower was sold in 1575 to one Thomas Eve, an
alderman of the Borough, and thus it came into the Corporation's
possession.

In 1887 the tower contained '... the police station, court rooms, and
council chamber, with portraits of Queens Elizabeth and Anne, King
Charles II and George III, and Dr Plume, a Maldon celebrity'. The clock,
illuminated and with chimes, costing £400, was presented to the town
in October 1881 by another of Maldon's MPs — George Courtauld.
Maldon's royal charter as a borough was granted first in 1171,
incredibly early, and in 1971 the 800th anniversary was proudly
celebrated, but there was a time between 1763 and 1810 when, through
illegality at elections, that charter was forfeited and its renewal cost
the burgesses £2,000!

MARGARETTING

Margaretting has much to commend it to the curious visitor. Not least its unusual name, which is explained by the dedication of its church to St Margaret, canonised in the 13th century. Trains on the main line to London rocket past it, yet the timbers of the wooden belfry have withstood the shock since the railway came in 1845. They were set up in the 15th century in an amazing network of beams and struts without the aid of brick or stone. The bells that hang there now all date from before the Reformation, the only complete ring in Essex to do so. Another feature worth noting is the east window. Though much restored it preserves some of the original Flemish glass which in beautiful colours sets out a simple family tree to show that Christ was descended from Jesse, father of David — a 'Jesse Window' in fact, a thing so rare now as to be remarkable.

In its suffused light, see the lectern which connects ancient with modern. It was presented to the church as a token of gratitude to God for their children by Mr and Mrs Allan Arthur who live in the village today. And that connects again with the Tanfield memorial over the north door, originally probably on a tomb chest which remembers John Tanfield, Catherine his wife and their seven children who prayed here early in the 17th century.

Margaretting Church Porch

MATCHING

Matching Hall and the Church of St Mary stand together far away from
the village of Matching Green up a long, narrow lane which is not a
through road. It is a peaceful place in an age of bustle. On the way, the
lane skirts a large lake on which hundreds of water fowl find food and
company, then it rises to pass a water-filled moat which laps at the foot of
a timber and plaster dovecote, a 400-year-old system for providing fresh
meat in winter when the beef and mutton ran out, for pigeons were kept
here by the score. It belongs to the Hall seen through the trees and is
probably contemporary with its timber construction.

Opposite stands St Mary's, amid oak and chestnut trees; for once the
fact that it is an almost complete rebuilding of 1875 hardly matters because
its setting is so superb, with its surviving 15th-century tower pushing up
through the trees behind an old house with jutting upper storey which
stands beside the churchyard fence. Until very recently the ground floor
of that house was lived in and a separate staircase gave access to the room
running the length of the upper storey. This is the famous 'wedding feast
house', so called because back in medieval days it was built by a man
named Chimney (and that is all that is known of him) to provide a large
room where poorer people might hold their wedding parties. Although
reported ruinous a hundred years ago, it has been sympathetically restored
and stands today as a beautiful tribute to an ancient act of charity.

Wedding Feast House

MERSEA ISLAND

There is only one road to Mersea, which has not really been an island ever since the Romans constructed the first causeway, now called The Street, a name which is actually an old world for the 'marshy land' which is crossed by the B1025! The oval island has but two settlements on it. East Mersea is the more remote and scattered. Though caravans have crept in to take advantage of the quieter patches of beach, the eastern part of the parish is protected as a Country Park. The church's massive stone tower, some five hundred years old, with its battlements and its stair turret jutting that little bit higher, made a fine mariners' mark in sailing days.

West Mersea is a different kettle of fish, having developed into quite a little holiday resort. We must blame the Romans for 'opening up' this island. They have caused quite a mystery here with their 22ft-high burial mound 100ft in diameter. Archaeologists did an awful lot of digging but found only the remains of a single cremation in a glass bowl in a casket contained in a tile-lined chamber just 18ins each way. The mystery deepened with the excavation of the 'wheel tomb' in the garden of a house nearby. It copied the mausoleums along the Appian Way with spoke-like walls radiating 30ft from a central structure to a perimeter wall high above the ground. Important people lived at Mersea but it keeps its secrets still.

Plan and reconstruction of Roman Wheel Tomb

MOUNTNESSING

Motorists on the B1002 (formerly the A12) have a clear view of an old
windmill on the rising ground above the Plough and the Prince of Wales
at Mountnessing. It makes such a pretty picture that it is hard to realise
that in its heyday it was simply a factory in the countryside, and noisy,
too, with the wind singing in the sails, the axles creaking and the stones
squealing their protest as the grain rattled down from the bin above while
the miller wearily humped the heavy sacks of flour to the door above the
long ladder.

So Mountnessing mill should be preserved as a reminder of a very basic
and vital Essex industry. Its very construction advertises another Essex
craft — timberwork building. Above the brick roundhouse, and built
around the great central baulk of timber, the mill was made so that it
could be turned round bodily, pivoting on that central post so that the
sails faced the wind. Even the drive and gears from sails to stones were
made of wood. Though a date has not been established it is thought
that the mill is three hundred years old. On reading the last county
directory published, for 1937, we find 'Agnis, Emily (Mrs) Miller
(Wind)'. In the following year the parish council was concerned to
restore it and in 1956 the County Council took on the responsibility
for its preservation.

NEWPORT

How did an inland village get such a name? It was one of the later Saxon settlements and was cleared from the forest as a 'new town' which is precisely what its name means. The Normans built a castle on the hill now occupied by the Grammar School, and Newport grew in size and importance with fairs and markets confirmed by charters dated from the 13th to the 15th centuries. Travellers along the great high road needed lodging and refreshment, bringing trade and prosperity, and buildings spread.

But harder times came when the Guildhall, or Town House, presented to the town by Robert Driver of Elmdon in 1544, stood empty and unused, where the Parish Rooms stand today. Its fate was bound up with that of Mrs Joyce Frankland, daughter of Robert Trappes, a wealthy London goldsmith. Twice the poor woman was widowed, and then her son died after falling from his horse. To console her, the Dean of St Paul's suggested that though she had lost one son she could gain many, and benefit them greatly, by endowing a school and involving herself in the lives of the scholars.

So in 1588, on the advice of a friend living locally, she started a school in that empty Guildhall, paying the master £20 a year. In 1837 the school was rebuilt on the same site, with room for sixty boys on the first floor, while the ground floor was rented out as a granary! In 1878 the present school was built. Over the years it has been much extended, including a Memorial Hall erected in 1920 to the memory of Old Newportonians who died in the war.

ORSETT

Down the lane opposite the big new hospital in Orsett stand two reminders of those days when this was a village unaffected by the bustle of cross-country traffic trying to beat the frustrations of the A13 to the south. One is the village 'cage', of 18th century origin, stoutly made of timber now blackened by time and weather. Here the hapless victim of drunkeness, the unruly lout or the petty thief languished in the greatest discomfort and smallest space until the village constable could arrange transport to trial in the nearest town. It was last used in 1846.

Beside it a fence encloses what looks like a bid for the record of the smallest field in England. It is the area of the original medieval 'pound' where animals which had strayed into the crops or down the street were impounded until claimed by their owners — who had to pay a fine to the Lord of the Manor in order to get their beasts back.

Further north, behind the houses, is an earthwork on which it is said the notorious Bishop Edmund Bonner, who ordered the execution of many Protestants in Mary Tudor's reign, had a Palace built.

PLESHEY 1

If a small Essex village was seen fit to be mentioned by William Shakespeare in one of his famous plays there must have been a good reason for it. It is that powerful people once lived in Pleshey. It looks small on the map today, but there is evidence in the earthworks, which enclose some 40acres, of occupation by Ancient Britons, who were ousted by the Romans sometime in the 1st century. Four hundred years later the Saxons settled here and called the place 'Tumblestoun' — town of tumuli or hills. They added the large moat within the outer-ring of defences. Then the Normans came and had their vassals heap up a huge, 50ft-high mound on which a motte-and-bailey — a palisaded yard with a wooden castle keep — was erected. Visitors can still stand on that lofty height and see a wide-spreading agricultural vista.

The bridge over which one crosses the moat was put up in the 15th century to a very unusual single-span design in brickwork. The castle was begun in 1140 by the famous Geoffrey de Mandeville and it is thus that the place got its present name of Pleshey — a Norman French idiom for a fortified place.

PLESHEY 2

The estate passed into the hands of the Duke of Gloucester, sixth son of Edward III and uncle of Richard II who was then on the throne. The King, fearful of his uncle's power visited him at Pleshey, lured him away from the security of his castle and had him murdered in 1397. So Shakespeare, following Froissart, makes his widow cry:

'With all good speed at Plashy visit me.
Alack, and what shall good old York there see
But empty lodgings and unfurnished walls,
Unpeopled offices, untrodden stones?
And what hear there for welcome but my groans?''
(Richard II, Act 1, Scene 2).

The village church, largely rebuilt in 1868, stands on the site of the chapel attached to a college for nine chaplains founded by the Duke of Gloucester in 1393, dissolved by Henry VIII and granted to Sir John Gate in 1546. The Lodge Farm was famous a century ago as a centre of agricultural technology. Here Thomas Churchman Darby built and tried out his first 'Darby Digger' which by means of steam did the work of about one hundred men. He was one of the experimenters who paved the way for today's mechanised agriculture, though his digger was not a complete success.

The House of Retreat in Pleshey was dedicated on 31st July 1919 by the first Bishop of Chelmsford. The building was put up in 1909 by the women of the Congregation of the Servants of Christ as their Hall of Prayer. Today this Church of England retreat houses 1500 guests a year in offering them a period of spiritual refreshment.

RAYNE

Rayne's claim to fame is not for what is, but for what might have been. There is an American museum which is that much richer at Rayne's expense. To clear up the mystery, walk into the church under the strong brick tower built around four hundred and fifty years ago at the expense of Sir William Capel, Lord Mayor of London and owner of the Hall. There you will find on show a knight's helm. It was worn by William's son Giles when he went to France as one of Henry VIII's courtiers who took part in the great jousting extravaganza at the Field of the Cloth of Gold in 1520. He must have done well, for he was knighted on the spot. His helm was remarkable at the time for the large number of openings (250) which pierced it to give it great vision while affording full protection, a break-through in the armour of the age.

He ordered that on his death it should be suspended above his tomb in keeping with the fashion of the times; and so it remained for nearly three hundred years right down to 1840. Then the church, except that wonderful tower, was in such a ruinous state that it was pulled down by builder William Parmenter who also broke up the Capel family tombs. Their stone went to make up the road to Rayne Mill, and that wonderful helm was found, one day, hanging from a peg in the builder's workshop.

The lady who found it bought it for a song from Parmenter and then gave or sold it to a friend, Baron de Cosson, an expert on armour. It disappeared and eventually turned up in the Metropolitan Museum of Art at New York, and they paid a high price for it.

So the parish of Rayne did not get a penny for its treasure, though the price it fetched would probably have paid for the restoration of the church. What it did receive in token of its loss was a replica of the real thing provided by the Museum, and looking at it I would say that nobody but an expert could tell the difference.

The full story of this attractive village has been told by the local branch of the WEA in its, *Rayne from early times to the present day.*

ROMFORD

As a town well outside London and quite separate for hundreds of years, Romford was granted a market as early as 1247, and though it is now just a part of the London Borough of Havering, housewives after a bargain still talk of going to Romford Market. Long may it keep that separate identity which can certainly still be found in the shadow of the big St Edward's Church, rebuilt in 1850, where the clock-ticking quietness under the 162ft spire contrasts with the raucous bustle of the market stretching all down the street. The stained glass window in the south aisle reminds us of the great brewing concern which has for so long brought employment and prosperity to the town, for it is in memory of Edward Ind JP who died in 1848, and he was one of the famous family now represented by the huge Ind Coope Brewery in modern buildings off the High Street.

A man who did not succeed in business and yet of whom Romford is very proud is Humphrey Repton 1752—1818, the great landscape gardener. He lost a fortune in two business ventures, then used his hobby of botany, applied it to gardening and recouped those losses in serving rich men as their landscape consultant for parks and gardens all over the country, including places in Essex like Rivenhall Place, Highams in Walthamstow, and Woodford Hall. For the last 45 years of his life he lived in a modest cottage at Hare Street, northeast of the town centre.

ROXWELL

Under Hroc, their leader, a little tribe of Saxons settled here beside the stream, the well, which made life possible, and by the 13th century it was being called Rokeswell. That spring still flows in the pond in the grounds of Broadgates, beside the church. The Roxwell brook runs behind the houses on the other side of the road, a small stream which can be very angry in flood. It kept the wheel of the watermill turning for hundreds of years, though its vagaries in drought and flood must have made the miller's life quite miserable. The mill continued working into the 20th century, but was adapted to steam and suffered an explosion which has taken its place in village folklore.

The official report shows that when John Shepherd Ray took over in 1868 the steam engine and its big brick chimney above a 12ft-high boiler were well-known features of the mill. On 5th February 1901 that boiler blew up with such fearsome force that it was catapulted 60ft into the road. On the way it smashed the beam engine, brought down a corner of the mill, shattered windows and yet miraculously injured no-one but the miller who was cut and scalded. He picked himself up, brushed himself off, and made those millstones whirl until 1926. Then it became obsolete and was used for all kinds of purposes until, in 1950, it was converted to an interesting house by a very unusual method. The old clapboard walls were simply sandwiched in two layers of concrete and that is why the doors and windows are all over the place — they were put in originally to suit the purpose of the mill.

SAFFRON WALDEN 1

The origin of Saffron Walden in prehistoric times is proved by the earth-works now called the Battle Ditches off Abbey Lane, which the Saxons used as a cemetery, but the real importance of the place stems from the castle and the great stone church built by the Normans and from the market literally 'pinched' from the then thriving Newport in 1141.

The big market place was divided into lanes lined with stalls, each row devoted to some particular ware — meat, bread, skins, clothing and so on. As the centuries passed the stalls became permanent structures, transformed into houses and shops lining very narrow streets. Butchers' Row still survives to give us the idea of how it all began, and even in the modern street arrangement of that area Saffron Walden is said to offer one of the best examples in England of the lay-out of a medieval market. As to the modern market place, I love the description in the town guide: 'The pillared and heavily classic Corn Exchange has a remarkable clock tower of indescribable design, facing the indescribable fountain in the middle of the square.' But in an age of box-like building I think those structures have real character.

SAFFRON WALDEN 2

This town achieved its name at two distinct periods. First its 'Walden'
denoted 'the valley of the Britons' as the Saxons described it when they
took over. Then 'Saffron' was used in cooking, dyeing and medicine
from medieval times and the saffron crocus bulbs were being grown all
around the town from very early times, though the first written record of
it is not until 1545 when the town is recorded as giving a gift of one pound
of saffron to 'my ladye Pagett', wife of a Secretary of State. Since it
took thirty thousand flower heads to make one pound of yellow saffron
that was a very generous gift.

But there is still a valued inheritance from those ancient British people
who had tilled the fields for centuries before the birth of Christ. They
needed to pacify their terrible gods to make life bearable. So they evolved
a strange dance on the green which has remained the Common to this day,
and the complicated patterns worn through the turf survived through
people's curiosity and children's sense of fun. In modern times, though,
the Maze as we now know it has had to be specially re-cut to ensure its
survival. Let us hope that the old god of fertility so earnestly invoked
by those ancient British farmers will continue to smile on Saffron
Walden's fields.

ST OSYTH

St Osyth is a village standing by one of the several creeks which form the river Colne, four miles west of Clacton. Its showpiece is the Priory which was founded around 1127 by Richard de Belmeis, Bishop of London, for the Augustinian order. The remains of that original building are slight, but there are some rooms in the present range of buildings which do date from the 13th century. It was in the 15th century that the gatehouse was built. Its splendid outward face is broad, three-storeyed and battlemented, patterned in flint and stone. It now houses a private collection of ceramics and jade which can only be viewed during the month of August.

Adaptations and extensions continued after the Priory, raised to Abbey status, was suppressed. Lord D'Arcy is said to have built the tower now crowned with an 18th-century lantern and clock, which rises behind the range of 16th-century gabled roofs of the inner courtyard. The gardens and the fragments of that original priory can be visited all through the summer.

The place itself gets its name from Osyth, the brave prioress of a nunnery raided by the Danes in 633. She was beheaded but, it is said, struggled to the church door carrying her head in her hands.

SOUTHEND-ON-SEA 1

With all the modern amenities, the new roads, the superior shopping facilities and the marvellous holiday attractions it offers one is tempted to say there is nothing old about Southend. Yet for those seeking the restful atmosphere of quiet old buildings there are pleasing places. One of them is the very heart of the borough, the Civic House, formerly 'Porters', a late 16th-century mansion in a beautifully kept garden. The Mayor entertains visitors here in rooms with linen-fold panelling and a fireplace which are part of the original building.

Even more peaceful, more wide-spreading are the gardens and the recreation grounds surrounding Prittlewell Priory, a 12th-century foundation of which the oldest surviving part is the refectory and the west range of the cloister including the Prior's rooms with a 15th-century roof. Much careful restoration has been carried out, including the marking out on the green lawn of the foundations of the church as discovered by recent excavation. The museum here illustrates life in South-east Essex throughout man's occupation.

And yet another old house in gardens enhanced by water features, relic of its ancient moat, is Southchurch Hall. It is a 13th- to 14th-century manor house of typical Essex timber construction, and very much worth visiting because its hall is one of the few still existing which are open to the roof as they were built. In recent years it has been transformed from a library to a museum of objects contemporary with the Hall, together with exhibition rooms.

SOUTHEND-ON-SEA 2

There is history behind the amusements which Southend offers to holiday-makers. The Kursaal Amusement Park's big dome erected in 1902 stands out against the tangle of steelwork of the switchback railway. Riders at the top of the death-defying dips have a grand view of the pier, claimed to be the longest in the world at over a mile-and-a-quarter. It has provided sea air and exercise for millions of people since it was completed in 1895, replacing the wooden structure, just as long, built in 1832 and later provided with 'a tramway for passengers to and from the steamers ...' which brought all the London trippers. The eastern arm of the extension was opened in 1929 by the Duke of Kent.

Such is its place in the Southend story that in 1971 it was listed for permanent preservation as a Class II building by the Department of the Environment. Disaster struck in July 1976 when part of the pier was consumed by fire. Repairs have been effected though the railway is not in action, so enthusiastic walkers can still patronise the pub, the amusements and the boats at the pier-head where the lifeboat station and the coast-guard look-out are objects of interest.

STANSTED MOUNTFITCHET

This place writes two chapters of its history simply in its name. When the Saxons came to clear living space in the woods they found the soil stony and gravelly and 'stone-place' they called it. Then the Normans were successful in their take-over bid and Stansted was one of fortyeight plums that fell into the lap of the Mountfitchet family, each one the Lordship of an Essex manor. They made their headquarters here and built a castle to uphold their ownership. Yet by 1258 the line failed and the castle crumbled — so completely that today only a few stones can be found on the castle mound with its moat ditch between the B1051 and the railway.

A later building which has survived as an interesting landmark is the windmill which was bought and given to the town by Lord Blyth. It is a tower mill in brick with most of its equipment in place, restored in recent years by great local effort and opened to the public.

The church of St Mary stands halfway between the town centre and the runways of Stansted airport; though rebuilt as time has demanded, its south doorway is magnificently Norman, and within are monuments to Sir Thomas Middleton, Lord Mayor of London, who died in 1631, and his daughter Hester. This family was Lord of the Manor through seven generations up to 1710.

STEEPLE BUMPSTEAD

Its first point of interest must be its name; the 'Steeple' referring to
St Mary's Norman tower, to distinguish it from its neighbour Helions
Bumpstead, though Norden the 16th-century map-maker says it is so
called because a steeple once crowned that tower and continues: 'Tis
otherwise styled Bumsted ad Turrim, at the Tower, from a Tower that
stood near the road leading from Haverill to Bathorne-bridge.' Bumpstead
is thought to indicate 'the place of reeds' which still grow in the stream
which trickles through the village on its way to the Stour.

The Moot Hall is the secular evidence of the continuity of life in this
place. Its position at the junction of the two main roads allows an
uninterrupted view of its exposed timber work with plaster infilling.
The ground floor, once open, has been filled in and a brick plinth supports
the shortened timbers, while a twin-shafted chimney stack has been added
early in its history. The projecting upper storey is supported on stout
timber brackets. Though it is recorded as being used as a school from
1592, it was built earlier than this and may well have been a guildhall
like that at Thaxted, or a wool or other market house like the one at
Horndon-on-the-Hill.

TENDRING

This small village achieves some distinction as the centre of a Hundred of parishes, as the base of a former Rural District Council, and as the name of the new District Council which embraces the coastal towns from Brightlingsea to Harwich. But its fame was of a different kind back in the 16th century. Then the area was so remote and the villagers so superstitious that whisperings of witchcraft reached the ears of constable and priest. The scare spread rapidly and in 1582 no less than thirteen women from this area were bound and carried off to Chelmsford to stand trial as witches. By our standards the evidence was unreliable and the sentences savage, for two of these poor old crones were hanged.

The reputation of the Tendring Hundred was remembered sixty years later by Matthew Hopkins, self-styled 'Witchfinder-General', a Manningtree lawyer who obtained a commission from Parliament to go on a witchhunting circuit. He and his men combed Tendring for witches before moving on to Suffolk. He used tricks to prove a woman's guilt and to wring a confession from her, for he was paid for this 'service' and more people were sent down to Chelmsford for trial and execution on his evidence in 1645.

THAXTED 1

Since several books could be written on the history of this world-famous Essex town on its own, any feature described in this kind of book must be considered simply as a single bead in a string of pearls. To enjoy the whole effect of that string one must visit the place.

The church is outstanding — in position a landmark for miles, in architecture five hundred years old and more, light and airy with a spire pointing up to a dizzy 181ft, its spirit captured by 'J.T.' writing in about 1900.

'Majestic giant! lordly spire!
What joys thy aspect doth inspire,
When absent long from home and thee,
Thy towering beacon first I see! ...'

Its big, clear glass windows give added grace to an interior which has been cleared of its heavy furniture, directing the eye to the beauty of its basic features, like the slim pillars of the 14th-century arcade, the figures on brackets and bosses, the very impressive carved wooden font case and cover originating in the 15th century.

It is hard to imagine the fuss and bother in the church when Cambridge under-graduates came down in a body to tear down the Sinn Fein flag and the red flag of communism which the colourful socialist preacher, Conrad Noel, hoisted in his church. He replaced them and burnt the Union Jack the undergraduates had put up with the aid of a long ladder borrowed from a local farmer, and with his friends he slashed the tyres of cars and motor cycles parked by the opposition in the Swan yard. That was in 1921: Noel continued as vicar here for 32 years, dying in 1942, and while he made Thaxted famous round the world for the Battle of the Flags, which inspired Robert Shaw to write his novel, *The Flag*, his wife made it renowned locally as the centre of the revival of the Morris dancing which is now such a popular tourist attraction.

THAXTED 2

Uttlesford District guide tells us: 'This former borough contains many picturesque old residences with fine timberwork.' We must pass them by appreciatively while making our way to that building, that timberwork which is Thaxted's glory. It is the Guildhall of course, very recently restored as near as possible to its original condition. It was built sometime in the 15th century as a meeting place for the merchant guild whose members safeguarded each others' interests in the market, which at this time in Thaxted was, rather unusually, largely concerned in a flourishing cutlery trade.

The cutlers were able to put up this stout, three-storeyed building, the ground floor open to the street with strong timbers taking the weight of the rooms above. Trading went on below and guild meetings above, where the two storeys jut out, one further than the other, under the twin, tiled, hipped roofs. From the streets which fork either side of it, little flights of steps give access to the trading floor. The brown timber and fawn plaster, the brackets on the strong uprights, the pointed arched windows, the heavy beams, all make a handsome monument of what those merchants simply considered a place of work.

When that trade declined William Benlowes, Serjeant at Law and Recorder for Thaxted, introduced cloth workers to diversify trade and maintain prosperity. He lived occasionally in the house near the Guildhall, now a restaurant, called the Recorder's House, and died in 1584. The Guildhall continued, being used for all manner of functions, from a jail on the ground floor to a meeting place for the town council above.

TILBURY

Tilbury may be best known today for its docks with five miles of deep water quays and all the latest handling systems for grain, timber, container and lorry traffic. But it also has its name in the history books for a very famous incident some four hundred years ago, when Queen Elizabeth came to show her support for her seamen and her troops when the Spanish Armada was on its way to batter them into submission in 1588. So it was in Essex, at Tilbury, that she uttered those stirring words: '... I am come amongst you as you see, at this time, not for my recreation and disport, but being resolved, in the midst and heat of the battle, to live or die amongst you all ... I know I have the body of a weak and feeble woman, but I have the heart and stomach of a king, and a king of England too, and think foul scorn that Parma or Spain, or any prince of Europe should dare to invade the borders of my realm ...' Such a momentous chapter in the story of Essex could not go unremarked. That is why, when the new County Council offices were built in the 1930s one of the walls of the large hall was entirely taken up with a mural depicting this event.

Elizabeth would have stood somewhere within the Fort which her father had built to protect traffic up the Thames and London itself from attack. The Fort which can now be visited by the public was built in the last quarter of the 17th century to replace that old blockhouse. Since great guns had by then become the main weapons, the fort had them mounted in embrasures with massive earthworks for protection and a walk around them offers fine views of shipping on the river, and of the neat old parade ground and buildings, busy with soldiers up to the last war when it received its share of bombs whilst being used by the Home Guard. In 1950 the War Department gave it to what is now the Department of the Environment 'for conservation and display as a national monument'.

WALTHAM ABBEY

Was King Harold buried in Waltham Abbey, now called the Abbey Church of Waltham Holy Cross and St Lawrence? We shall never know, but the legends persist and a possible site is marked. The Abbey, the whole town, got its name from a great wooden cross which Tovi, standard bearer to King Canute, said he found on his land in Somerset. He was directed to bear it as far as this place where he had a church built to house it; on the other hand it may have been named after the Eleanor Cross erected just over the county border. However, it is said that Harold, then but an Earl, was healed of paralysis at that cross in the church, so he determined to honour it. His huge and beautiful church was completed in 1060, far bigger than that we see today and it was further extended and beautified as a great monastery by King Henry II, to reach Abbey status in 1184.

All was brought to nought by Henry VIII's edict of dissolution. The Abbey passed into private hands and was to be totally demolished, but the townspeople claimed that part of the nave built for Harold's early church as their place of worship — and it was saved for them. But in 1552 the tower at the east end fell down, causing a great deal of damage. A very good guide is available in the church which details a hundred remarkable features, from the Denny tomb of 1600 to the fresco of the Last Supper or the great rose window designed by Sir Edward Burne-Jones in 1861.

Go outside and in the turf under that same window you will see the simple stone which now marks the place where King Harold is said to have been buried — surely a milestone in British history.

WITHAM

What a blessing it was when the A12 was diverted away from this town.
Today the spreading industrial estate reaches to the bypass itself and the
population has so increased that natives are thin on the ground. But there
are places where the old Witham peeps out; not least in the upper storeys
of the bright new stores in the High Street which show how the houses
were 'done up' with new facades in Georgian times, for then it was that
great hopes were entertained of establishing a fashionable spa here. A
chalybeate spring was 'discovered' but either the state of the roads and
the distance from London or the competition from other more quickly
developed watering places doomed the project from the start, and Witham
went on slowly but profitably as a small market town in a good farming
area.

Its older history is to be read in the name of its Chipping Hill and the
Church of St Nicholas upon it. A 'cheaping' was a Saxon market and
this quiet spot was once the busiest and noisiest in Witham. The Anglo-
Saxon Chronicle mentions that, '... the earthwork at Witham was being
built and stockaded ...' in 913 AD, and that mound can be detected today
near the station, bisected by the railway. Local historian Maurice Smith
writes: 'Motorists when emerging from The Avenue and Avenue Road
fail to realise that the steep slope they have to negotiate is the relic of the
defensive bank of the ancient fortification.'

The Old Forge, Chipping Hill

WIVENHOE

Wivenhoe is two-faced. It looks forward with the University of Essex established in its Park since 1964, and with its facilities for yachting, boating and fishing, including the famous Nottage Institute of seamanship founded in 1895. And it looks backward to the days when a man was educated only to a craft, like pargetting, or a craftiness, like smuggling. The pargetting, ornamental plaster work, is to be seen in a richness un-equalled in Essex on the walls of the 17th-century, timber-framed Garrison House in East Street. The smugglers are supposed to have used it at one time as a kind of retail warehouse for all that French brandy and lace. The Colne was quiet enough then for a small boat to slip quickly up to the quay and no questions asked. That Quay still fascinates with marine activity and looks much the same as in those exciting days, yet it was severely damaged in the great Essex earthquake of 1884 and Quayside Cottage had to be rebuilt. Alongside it Maple Cottage, and, further on, Trinity House, are scheduled for preservation.

The sailors' landmark has always been the tower of St Mary's, built around 1500, off the High Street just above the quay. It, too, suffered from the Earthquake, and had to be restored, but it keeps two lovely big brasses, of 1507 to William Viscount Beaumont, and of 1537 to his widow Elizabeth who died wife of the Earl of Oxford.

Garrison House, Pargetting

126

WOODHAM FERRERS

That 'Ham' in the 'wood' covered a wide area at the Conquest when one-third of it was granted to Henry de Ferrers. Visible history begins in the 13th century with the church of St Mary where the wooden turret with its one bell reminds us that the original tower fell down in 1703. The next tower also collapsed, so the villagers gave up and the great tower arch was blocked up. Above the chancel arch a 15th-century wall painting tells the story of the day of reckoning to a congregation which could not read or write. An unexpected and moving monument is that erected in 1619 to Cecilie, widow of the Archbishop of York. Her effigy kneels in an allegorical scene, virtually embowered in beautifully carved roses. The Archbishop inherited land here and around 1576 built the big house now called Edwin's Hall (he was Edwin Sandys), which is reputed to be haunted.

More prosaic, far more ancient, are the mounds still visible just under two miles southeast of the church on the edge of the creek. They are the remains of the prehistoric craft of boiling sea water to produce salt which continued into the 18th century, and a farm, and a new estate are called Saltcoates after these workings. It was the opening of the Great Eastern branch line through here in 1889 which caused rapid development of the southern end of the parish, with land speculation causing a blight of the countryside divided into miserably equipped 'smallholdings'.

It was not until 1971 when the County Council published an 'Appraisal' of South Woodham Ferrers that the process of planned re-development began and a 'new town in the country' was mooted. Today, with a huge superstore complex and houses springing up almost overnight South and North Woodham have become divorced. The town grows and grows in the south, and to the north the old houses, the church, the pub and the post office heave a sigh — and sleep again.

Superstore, South Woodham Ferrers

127

WRITTLE

Here is a happy place with which to end a book. One fine parish church, two village greens, three pleasant pubs around them and any number of houses jostling for space in an architectural variety which speaks of the long history of the place. Yet the most picturesque part, the village pond at the foot of the green, is a product of the machine age, for it came into being as a source of water for those thirsty traction engines. The traffic now is lighter in weight, heavier in volume, but the ducks quack and splash unconcernedly.

All round the larger green are gems of architecture, just plain homes to the people who live in them, from the big old houses on the south side, to the smaller houses and shops to the north where there are two houses built of stone, very unusual in Essex. They are the remains of the original church tower. In 1802 it fell down, bells and all.

Writtle's name has gone round the world for its place in the world-shrinking miracle of radio. Yet Marconi's research establishment is tucked away unobtrusively at the far corner of the lower, St John's, green where it has been since the beginning of the century. It is said that it was sited here because the aerials needed just the level ground furnished by the plain of the river Wid. From here public wireless transmission was beamed across the continent when the Postmaster-General allowed the resumption of the service to 'amateurs' from 14th February 1922.